SOUL ALERT

Thriving Spiritually as Aliens and Strangers in the World

D1402222

Karen Mains

Mainstay Church Resources
Wheaton, Illinois

Soul Alert: Thriving Spiritually as Aliens and Strangers in the World

Copyright © 2002 by Karen Burton Mains

All rights reserved.

Cover Designer: Esther Wodrich
Cover Design Brainstorm Team: Peder Gulbrandsen, Jennifer
 Knaak, Patric Knaak, Gary G. Petro, Craig Shelbrock,
 Caleb Spencer, Esther Wodrich
Interior Designer: Andrea Reider
Editor: Laurie Mains

Vision of Mainstay Church Resources: In this sight and sound
culture, our holy task is to encourage pastors and all people in
their spiritual journeys through innovative life-application
resources that transform Sunday and every day into significant
growth experiences with the risen Christ. To support this vision,
Mainstay Church Resources provides practical tools and
resources, including the annual 60-Day Spiritual Adventure, the
Seasonal Advent Celebration, and the Pastor's Toolkit.

Visit our website at www.teamsundays.org/adventure.

MAINSTAY
*The Leader in
Sunday Solutions*

ISBN 1-57849-264-5
Printed in the United States of America
05   04   03   02   01   5   4   3   2   1

Contents

Travels in Foreign Lands: A Word from a Spiritual Alien

Hear my prayer, O Lord, listen to my cry for help; be not deaf to my weeping. For I dwell with you as an alien, a stranger, as all my fathers were.

—Psalms 39:12

IF THE Christian life is a pilgrimage, then any journey can become a metaphor that teaches powerful truths.

This became glaringly true to me when I traveled on my own through Europe for a month. Though I have landed in many corners of the earth over the last 20 years, this was the first journey through foreign lands I made unaccompanied by a host skilled in translating the language and interpreting the culture for me. I discovered that travel of any kind, even when it is not conducted through hostile territory, holds the possibilities for amazing growth as well as the potential for imminent peril.

Journey experiences, of course, parallel the Christian passage as outlined in various pilgrimage literature—from the Old Testament account of Israel's flight out of Egypt and the 40 formative years in the wilderness to the missionary journeys in the New Testament; from the frequent biblical reminders that we are indeed "strangers and pilgrims on the earth" to the many religious writings such as John Bunyan's classic allegory *Pilgrim's Progress* or the great contemporary trilogy by J. R. R. Tolkien, *The Lord of the Rings*. All of these writings warn us about the perils of transit, to our souls as well as to our bodies, but they also propose intriguing opportunities for doing more than surviving the journey. They give us glimpses of greatness, of noble deeds, of heroes and heroines who thrive spiritually.

My unaccompanied journey began with an invitation from the Protestant Women of the Chapel of the United States Armed Forces in Europe. Would I speak at a five-day retreat held at the Sauerland Stern, a resort tucked at the foot of the Ettlesberg mountains above the little cure spa of Willingen, Germany? How could I possibly *not* avail myself of such a privileged opportunity? Of course I would come.

After totaling the proposed honorarium with the generous travel allowance, it dawned on me that with a Eurail pass and much mooching off hospitable friends and their families, I could underwrite the expenses for a four-week trip on the Continent. Oh, I'd been to Europe before, if you could call it that. I'd sat on runways on my way to Israel or while returning from a seven-week journey along the Pacific Rim; I'd touched European soil in Amsterdam and Vienna, used the bathrooms during a brief layover at Charles de Gaulle International in Paris, stayed one night in Rome on a sleepover . . . but I had never had an opportunity to submerge myself for even a day as a tourist in the great cultures of Europe.

So I spun a silver travel cobweb for David, my husband, to accompany me. He informed me that he couldn't possibly get away from his national religious media responsibilities in November and December, the months of my projected travel. As much as I tried, I couldn't find female companionship. Obviously, a choice lay before me. I could play it safe—maybe stay a few extra days sightseeing in Germany with my hostess. Or I could seize the moment and take what felt like a risky journey, the opportunity for which might never come my way again.

I decided I did not want to end my days thinking, *Why didn't I grab that chance to see Europe when it came my way?* So I contacted any friends who had ever blithely extended invitations to me, "If you're ever in Florence (or Madrid or Paris or London), come stay with us." Setting off to explore, I felt like a solo Dona Quixota without a female sidekick, a Sancha Panza.

My week of speaking ministry in Germany was joyful labor, but when my hostess, Nancy Hagen, an Army chaplain's wife serving as the European Council President for the Protestant Women of the Chapel, put me on the train in Frankfurt to travel to Florence with a breathlessly brief stop to change lines in Basel, Switzerland, I felt panic rise. It was there that I, a woman who has gone through most of life without compulsive fears, began to empathize deeply with friends who manage chronic anxiety attacks. Would I have enough time to change trains? How, without an interpreter, would I find the right track, the right car, the right numbered seat? Could I make my way through conversations in the various Romance languages—Italian, Spanish, French—with only my spotty high-school Latin and rusty college French? Would I have the right coinage in the right exchange? Would my hosts (some I had never met) actually greet my train at its destination? What if someone stole my wallet (or my passport or my traveler's checks)?

This mounting anxiety was not helped by the fact that my concerned adult children had briefed me on the dangers of solo travel overseas. The horror stories abounded. Nor did the travel section of the Chicago newspaper help, with its statistics of petty thievery overseas: "Some 1,265 stolen U.S. passports per 783,592 tourists in Madrid and Barcelona; 1,331 stolen U. S. passports per 1,210,390 tourists in Rome, Milan, and Florence; 1,053 stolen U.S. passports per 1,968,000 tourists in Paris." Terrifying indeed!

I hid half my traveler's checks in a boot I was wearing, another packet in my undergarments; my passport was plunged deep into my purse, which I clutched to my side at all times, and my Eurail tickets were tucked in a suitcase pocket. Unfortunately, I kept forgetting where I'd put what! Experience also began to teach me that, despite what flippant Americans vow, all Europeans do *not* speak English. Most, in no matter what language, "speek very leetle."

Believe me, I thought often about how Scripture compares the spiritual journey to that of travelers navigating foreign territory. During those long train hours traveling—from Frankfurt down through the Alps to Florence, then to Madrid (with changeovers in Milan and Barcelona), Paris, and finally, London—I seriously considered the Christian pilgrimage.

After commending the heroes and heroines of faith, the writer of Hebrews reminds us,

> All these people were still living by faith when they died. They did not receive the things promised; they only saw them and welcomed them from a distance. And they admitted that they were aliens and strangers on earth. People who say such things show that they are looking for a country of their own. If they had been thinking of the country they had left, they would have had opportunity to return. Instead, they were longing for a better country—a heavenly one. Therefore God is not ashamed to be called their God, for he has prepared a city for them.   Hebrews 11:13–16

Because I was traveling by myself and not relaxing under the protective hospitality of a skilled travel guide, my opportunities for personal growth were huge. I learned how to make my way alone in a foreign city. I learned which directions were where in Europe.

I learned how to use the phone. In Barcelona, while changing trains for Madrid, four separate nationals responded to my broken Spanish with their broken English and instructed me how to place a long-distance call to my friends in Madrid who were waiting for news of my final arrival time. But each stranger instructed me in a contradictory method of long-distance phoning! By the time I finally reached the Krachts, my mind had become one frightful mixture of confused languages. "Hello, Doug," I said into the receiver. "This is Karen Mains. I am in Barce*noble.*" This man—a missionary for years in Spain and used to the exertions of cross-cultural living, even at the elementary levels I was encountering—had the grace to laugh. For a moment, his lightheartedness alleviated my multiplying feelings of incompetence.

It is true: Journeys that require risks of any kind will produce growth in the riskers who take them. I learned how to read a train schedule in a foreign language, how to find the departure time, the right track, the train car, the seat, and what to do with my luggage. I learned where to exchange money and how to use exchange machines and where to find the best rate of exchange.

But why was I still so panicky—all the time? Well, a parallel truth also crowds the growth curves travel forces upon us. Journeys that require risks of any kind can be fraught with danger. I could lose my way, my money, and my passport, becoming an absolute stranger without knowledge of the native language and with no human aid, should I make a wrong choice.

I obsessively read and reread the train schedules, marking off the names of places as I passed, counting out how many stops before my destination. Simply, I was coping with fear—pure travel terror. I, who prided myself on my independence and self-sufficiency, didn't really know where I was going or exactly how I was going to get there or what would happen if I made a mistake along the way. It was this heading into the unknown that was throwing me into anxiety compulsions I could scarcely control. *(Where did you hide your traveler's checks? Keep an eye on your luggage; count the pieces. Check your tickets; reread the schedule. . . . Is anything missing?)*

Obviously, when I reached my destinations, those familiar faces of the Hagens in Germany, Doug and Jeremy and Aleene Kracht in Spain, Sue Clifton of Institut Biblique Europeen in France brought me enormous relief. Immediately, my responsibility for language and currency and schedules and place names were transferred to my hosts and hostesses. My vulnerability was suddenly lifted from my shoulders. And in that release, I began to process my personal traveler's malady. My anxious behavior indicated that I believed the responsibility for my transit weighed solely on my own shoulders. We live what we believe: Though a Christian, I was making a journey across Europe as a non-Christian. I did not trust God to be my travel companion.

Watching the countryside whizzing past the train windows or lying awake on the top bunk of a sleeping compartment, wondering how on earth I was going to move my two large suitcases, satchel, and purse between trains in the time allotted during the next day's changeover (this was another problem—due to my speaking assignment for 700 women at the beginning of the journey, I had to drag extra baggage with me for the rest of my travels), somewhere along the way I began to ask: If I believed God was the One who had graciously made this journey possible, couldn't I also believe he was in charge of my travel itinerary?

Could I choose to believe he would get me where I needed to go without harm? Could I trust him to nudge me when I needed to disembark or to help me find my way if I made a mistake? If I could relax instantly when I laid eyes on the face of familiar friends, couldn't I also relax when I turned the gaze of my soul toward God? In fact, wasn't the Lord my Holy Conductor? My Tour Leader? Wasn't he also my Divine Translator? Did I really think I was journeying alone?

Where was the exercise of my Christian belief system during the course of this journey? I could speak to 700 women about knowing the Presence of God in their lives; I just couldn't practice it when journeying alone across foreign territory! Though I have circled the world in the company of many veteran travelers, this solo journey across Europe forced me to understand that a spiritual metaphor existed between my travel and the compulsive anxiety that raised its ugly head to torment me.

I faced an awful truth: Though I could trust God in the familiar and comfortable, I had pragmatic difficulties applying faith disciplines to a pilgrimage across territory that was unknown and potentially hostile, even life-threatening.

This lack in myself was a truth I desperately needed to correct, as over the next seven years I faced extreme circumstances that threatened the health of my family, my reputation, and the future of our ministry. I was to stare at the sudden loss of all material security and my own consequent inadequacies in the face of circumstances I had never before encountered.

These travel lessons, learned while crossing Europe alone, have stood me in good stead both physically and spiritually ever since. I now know God allowed the difficult journey of the years that were to come for the growth of my soul; indeed, the positive opportunities that present themselves in desperate circumstances are enormous. It is he who keeps warning and guarding me against the imminent perils that also surround me on all sides. The dangers to my soul are real in this lifelong passage. I have become dependant upon him to alert me to the dual possibilities of growth and imminent peril in my human journey upon the earth.

Adventure Traveling

This book, *Soul Alert: Thriving Spiritually as Aliens and Strangers in the World,* applies the metaphor of travel to the Christian pilgrimage. We at Mainstay Ministries provide this Guidebook for everyone going on the 50-Day Spiritual Adventure entitled *More than Survivors: What It Takes to Thrive Spiritually.*

The 50-Day Adventures look simple, but they are more difficult than they at first appear. In fact, we at

Mainstay have found that adventurers need as much accountability as possible to complete the daily journal exercises. Just as I felt more comfortable in my traveling when I had friends to help me, you will enjoy the Adventure more if you have others to share the experience. So try to establish an ongoing connection within the community of faith—a small group such as an adult Sunday School class or a weekly time of sharing the Adventure with one other person or several friends. Families with children or grandparents and grandchildren can encourage spiritual growth in one another through the age-graded Adventure journals. Also, our website, www.team-sundays.org/adventure, posts daily messages to help keep you on track.

One of the greatest flaws of North American Christians is that we are becoming a generation of people whose belief system doesn't match our behavior. Unknowingly, we are being secularized. The recent studies of the Barna Research Group indicate that there is little significant difference between evangelical Christians and the rest of society. In a nationwide survey among born-again adults, none of the individuals interviewed said that the single, most important goal in their life was to be a committed follower of Jesus Christ. Born-again Christians spend seven times as many hours on entertainment as they do on spiritual activities. Less than one-third of all young people are likely to attend a Christian church once they are living on their own.

These results should flash the soul alert. We need to post "Danger Ahead" signs! We are drifting toward nominal Christianity, traveling through life calling ourselves followers of Jesus Christ but not living in a radically Christian manner. Spiritually, North America is quickly becoming the next Europe.

In his book *The Spirit of the Disciplines,* Dallas Willard offers an important analysis for the prevailing powerlessness of the modern church. First, he writes, the church "must take the need for human transformation as seriously as do modern revolutionary movements." He continues,

> The modern negative critique of Christianity arose in the first place because the church was not faithful to its own message—it failed to take human transformation seriously as a real, practical issue to be dealt with in realistic terms.

Willard's second point about the failure of the contemporary church is as important as the first:

> It needs to clarify and exemplify realistic methods of human transformation. It must show how the ordinary individuals who make up the human race today can become, through the grace of Christ, a love-filled, effective, and powerful community.[1]

This travel across life is not a pleasure cruise for the Christian. The soul of the church in contemporary western culture is in danger. We are allowing ourselves to be assimilated. There is little essential difference between us and the society that surrounds us. In fact, we long to be like the world. Soul alert! Realistic and practical human transformation is no longer the ideal! While traversing this foreign culture, a thieving enemy is pinching our heavenly papers, and we are in danger of losing our distinctive identity as strangers and aliens in the world.

The 50-Day Spiritual Adventure *More than Survivors: What It Takes to Thrive Spiritually* and this companion Guidebook, *Soul Alert,* are designed to stimulate human transformation. Each chapter contains some or all of these components:

1. *A Character Hero*—an example of a biblical hero or heroine who thrived spiritually as a stranger and alien in a hostile culture.

2. *Travel Wisdom*—a look through the lens of travel or immigration in order to clarify our own understanding of what it means to be spiritual strangers and aliens on the earth.

3. *Application Step*—a practical way to use a theological truth to transform daily living.

4. *Reality Checkpoints*—a few questions designed to challenge the cultural assimilation we often don't realize is happening.

My prayer for you during this Adventure is that, although travel across foreign territory is often filled with peril, you will find the opportunities for growth exciting and life changing. We at Mainstay want you to be more than survivors. You can learn to thrive spiritually as aliens and strangers in the world. Have a remarkable Spiritual Adventure!

CHAPTER 1

Moses: The Wonder-Working Wanderer

THEME
Practice Making Soul-Conscious Choices

TEXT
Hebrews 11:24–28

APPLICATION 1
Critique Your Choices

T HE AMAZING thing about wilderness wanderings is that our souls often flourish in parched and arid terrain; whereas when we are comfortable, protected by familiarity and surrounded by the pleasures and treasures of home, our souls tend to languish.

Moses—the well-bred, adopted son of Pharaoh's daughter who was credited by the martyr Stephen with being highly educated and having the qualities of a born leader (Acts 7:22)—this Moses flees to the wilderness of Midian.

Knowing something about the effect of dual citizenships and the identity conflict this can cause, we might surmise that Moses' flight was catalyzed by such a crisis. Oh, certainly, he was fleeing for his life, but what led him to abandon the privileges of being an Egyptian? At some point, Moses becomes indignant about the treatment of his own race, the Hebrew people who have become slaves. Somewhere, Moses realizes that he has been snatched from the jaws of an edict issued by his adoptive grandfather, the infanticide of male babies. When he is forty years of age, his indignation is so complete that Exodus 2:11 tells us, "He went out to his people and looked on their burdens." An Egyptian is beating a slave. Enraged, Moses murders the tormentor, secretly hiding the body in the sand.

The identity conflict unfolds the very next day. Two Hebrews slaves are fighting with each other.

When Moses attempts to end the fisticuffs, the wrongdoer turns and taunts him with knowledge of what he thought was secret violence: "Who made you a prince and a judge over us? Do you mean to kill me as you killed the Egyptian?" (vs. 14). No matter how much indignation Moses exercises, nothing in his ruling class sphere has prepared him to deeply empathize with the inhuman degradation of a slave nation; he has been a defender for them, and this man is spitting in his face. Privilege separates Moses, as it does all of us, from oppressed brethren. He may be a Hebrew genetically; he is not one mentally. This rabble-rouser senses the disparity. The process of stripping away the mental blind-cloths due to privilege is a matter for years, for decades, not one for days or weeks.

Pharaoh, infuriated, puts out the word that it's past time to activate that previous death edict. Moses flees to the wilderness of Midian to preserve his life, but in God's amazing provision, the wilderness preserves Moses' soul. It is in the desert that Moses begins to comprehend the national identity of the Hebrews. More importantly, he comes to know the One who is the God of the Hebrew people.

In the wilderness there is time enough for transformation, 40 years to be exact. Forty years for the wasteland and the vast expanse of space, for the thought-provoking arches of day and night skies to challenge him with the majesty and wonder of creation.

Forty years for the crafty skill of herding and tending hundreds of head of livestock to change him from a learned effete to a workingman. How amazing that the man who becomes Moses' father-in-law is a priest of Midian, a holy man concerned about things sacred. Time enough for a decades-long dialogue profound enough to determine the nature of this one true God. In Egypt, the religion was a complex polytheism, with many local deities up and down the land. Eventually, in the succession of royal dynasties, cosmic deities emerged: Ra, the sun-god; Nut the sky-goddess; Shu, Geb, and Nu, the gods of air, earth, and the primordial waters; then the great cult of Osiris, his wife, Isis, and their son, Horus.

Forty years are needed, and the thousands of empty miles traversed on foot, for the flaming sun to burn up, bleach out, blaze away the Egyptian thinking that has subsumed Moses' mind. Forty years to learn the terrain around the Gulf of 'Aqabah and to unlock the secrets of the desert so that he can thrive and lead a slave nation (some 600,000 men plus women and children) through another 40 years of nomadic vagabondage in order for their subservient mentalities to be burned up, bleached out, blazed away. Forty years for this half-prince of Egypt to take on the identity of a wanderer who will become a wonder-worker.

Moses marries Zipporah, the daughter of Jethro—that holy man of Midian—and sires a son. He names the child *Gershom,* saying, "I have become an alien in a foreign land." This may have been a lament, a poor-me-so-far-away-from-home disposition, but what if it was not? What if it was a mnemonic devise? What if the brilliant future law-maker and judge, genius theologian, and organiza-tional mastermind was reminding himself of a truth he was just beginning to grasp, a truth essential to his future path, to his very survival? Soon the great I AM would call him to go forward and not look back. Moses needed to remember, for the sake of over 1 million straggling, difficult, contrary people and their role in God's grand scheme of redemption, that they were heading toward a better place, a promised land, a far-off country of milk and honey.

Each time he took the wiggling baby into his arms or breathed the name, "Gershom! Gershom!" Each time they played hide-and-seek around his father-in-law's tent flaps, each time he whispered a prayer over the dear little body or a blessing on the curling hair of his growing son. Each time he called that name as they herded flocks ("This way, Gershom, my son") or called out in dismay, "Oh Gershom!" Each time he shouted, thinking the youth had wandered too far, and the hills echoed the call, "Gersho-o-o-m! Gersho-o-o-m!" . . . Moses remembered: *I am not an Egyptian. I am an alien and stranger in this world.*

Scripture teaches that any culture a Christian crosses is foreign land. This reality also is essential to our survival as Christ-followers. We cannot be used by God as change-agents in the world if we have become too attached and have lost sight of the heavenly destination. Nor can we profit if we long for the pleasures and treasures of the surrounding society and are confused because of our dual citizenship, or love our privileges so much we cannot empathize with the hoards oppressed by a violent enemy who is committed to their spiritual genocide. God cannot use us if we are not prepared to flee to the wilderness so he can strip our minds and grow our souls.

It may come as a shock to some, but Christianity has always valued those who denied themselves this world's goods for the sake of a higher cause. The monastic vows of poverty, chastity, and obedience, in whatever form, are still the great antidotes for a sickly Christianity that values comfort over holiness and considers high qualifications for spiritual leadership to include a fat and well-managed financial portfolio.

It will take years to achieve the necessary spiritual alien mentality. It took Moses forty. A 50-Day Spiritual Adventure will not be long enough; this is just a start. We can help things along, however, by memorizing some of the passages from Scripture that emphasize our status as strangers and aliens. A good place to start is 1 Peter 2:9–12:

> But you are a chosen people, a royal priesthood, a holy nation, a people belonging to God, that you may declare the praises of him who called you out of darkness into his wonderful light.

Once you were not a people, but now you are the
people of God; once you had not received mercy,
but now you have received mercy.

Dear friends, I urge you as aliens and strangers
in the world, to abstain from sinful desires, which
war against your soul. Live such good lives among
the pagans that, though they accuse you of doing
wrong, they may see your good deeds and glorify
God on the day he visits us.

Without a doubt, Moses is a national and spiritual hero. Jewish people today look to him as a historical figure without precedent. The book of
Hebrews applauds him for his exercise of faith.
Moses understands that he is not a citizen of Egypt.
Exile in the wilderness has done its good work in
him, but in order to be more than a survivor, Moses
has to make soul-conscious choices.

What are soul-conscious choices? Soul-conscious
choices are those that consider if what we do or
what we don't do will affect the condition of our
souls, negatively or positively. Small choices made in
the present often have enormous impact, for good or
ill, down the road. Soul-conscious choices demand
that we stay alert, pay attention to how our decisions
form our spiritual center. It is a way of living unto
God that is not careless about how we conduct our
sojourn while traveling through the foreign territory
of life.

Travel Wisdom

In nations like the United States and Canada, which have been established on the longings of immigrants through decades of history, we attempt to describe ourselves as a "melting pot" or a "tossed salad" or a "stir fry" of different peoples. Although many of us are familiar with the periodic waves of immigration that have occurred, bringing different nationalities to our shores, most of us are less familiar with the ongoing struggles of immigrants today. While illegal immigration remains an extremely contentious issue, let's look for a while at soul-consciousness through the lens of the illegal alien.

What is it all immigrants want?

That's a simple question to answer. What would *you* want? They want to leave their country. They want to find shelter and get a job so they have income. They want to procure the legal papers that will allow them to stay, to travel, to find work.

In the eyes of the U.S. Immigration and Naturalization Services (INS), there are basically five categories of people in the world:

1. *You have received citizenship and are now a naturalized U.S. citizen.* This means citizenship has been conferred at birth, acquired through your parents' citizenship, or obtained by naturalization, usually after five years as a resident.

2. *You are a legal alien.* This means you have the right to live and work permanently in the U.S. while still a citizen of another country. (You hold the fabled "green card"—which in its present incarnation is actually off-white with a magnetic strip.)

3. *You are temporarily in the U.S. on a non-immigrant visa.* Example of such visas are the B-2 visitor visa issued for business or pleasure, the F-1 student visa for study, or the H-1B visa issued to workers in specialty occupations.

4. *You are a refugee or an asylee.* You must prove a "well-founded fear of persecution," which is subjectively genuine and objectively reasonable.

5. *You are an undocumented illegal.*[1]

The major concern for members of this fifth category, who generally cannot receive a non- immigrant visa, is to achieve legal status or a "green card." They want to work legally. And here is where those soul-conscious choices come in.

For three to five years, a Mexican family was part of the migrations that fill the labor shortage of low-paying jobs in construction, landscaping, service industries, taxi and factory enterprises, and so on. (Despite the outcry about Mexican workers, the two nations have developed a symbiotic economic relationship. Mexico profits from the income for its often impoverished worker classes, and the States are supplied with field hands, janitors, landscape workers, nurses' aids, and other service workers.) Instead of returning home, because they had housing and work, this family brought their children up from south of the border. Years have passed, and they can't find any way to legalize their status.

The wife, a factory employee, heard of some guy working out of his house who said he's a notary of the public. In Mexico, *notoria publica* is a high level lawyer. A friend on the assembly line reported, "I have a cousin who got legal papers through this *notoria.*"

The wife talked it over with her husband, "Sure, go ahead. What have we got to lose?" But she was uneasy and suspicious after her appointment. The man was disorganized, rude, seemed uneducated. He wanted $2,000 up front for the family and $4,000 to close the deal. He had her fill out papers, asked for their birth and marriage certificates, and kept these original documents (which, in Mexico, can be difficult to procure). Despite her inner cautions, they gave the man the money and, sure enough, in a few months, she had work authorization, and they received social security cards.

One year passed, and it was time to renew the work authorization. The wife went to the Chicago immigration office, but they took away her card and would not renew it. She was alarmed and highly concerned, so she called the notary. His phone was disconnected and there was no way to reach the man. She inquired around, discovered this shark had been booked on charges of fraud. Meanwhile, he

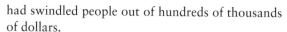

had swindled people out of hundreds of thousands of dollars.

One day, this family received a letter from INS, written in English. They couldn't understand what it said, except that it had a date on it and a time. While shopping in a Mexican grocery store in her neighborhood, the wife and mother noticed a community organization flyer written in Spanish that offered to help with immigration problems. She took her letter, and a lady kindly explained that she had been defrauded. They had lost $6,000. The letter was a notice to appear in court in a month, when they would be deported for being in the States illegally and for procuring illegal papers. If the woman didn't appear, they would be deported *in absentia* and a serious black mark would appear on her record for years to come.

Scenarios like this push immigration specialists to continually remind the people who come for help, "Think. Use your head! If it were that easy, wouldn't *everyone* have their papers?" This is the first (though not necessarily most important) question you need to consider when making a soul-choice: What is the logical outcome? Does it really make sense to follow this course of action? We have to be alert about making decisions that may eventually offend what we know to be right and true. Choices made today can have profound detrimental effect on our spiritual state tomorrow. So, in addition to these questions, be sure to ask yourself how a decision or response or situation will affect your soul.

While talking with the community organizer, the Mexican woman said that she thought something was fishy; intuitively, she knew something was wrong. Here is my second point: Follow your intuition. If the kingdom of God is within you (Luke 17:21), if you truly are the temple of the Holy Spirit (1 Corinthians 6:19), if, as children say, Jesus lives in your heart, then you can begin to listen to the Word speaking inside.

Do you feel uncomfortable? A good soul-conscious choice may be to get out of the situation. Do you feel you should say something, even though you may lose the respect of your peers? Possibly God is providing a circumstance for you to learn humility. Listen to your conscience as the voice of God. If our Mexican friend—with whom now we all can sympathize, because we also sometimes disregard that feeling of uneasiness—had listened to the inner voice, the feeling of suspicion, she might have been saved. We, too, will be saved from many soul-damaging decisions if we learn to listen and obey.

Here is a third caution: Try not to procrastinate. Sometimes we err through simple neglect; we let things happen to our souls without exercising any intentional decision-making process. As the saying goes, not to decide is to decide.

Application Step: Critique Your Choices

Scripture says that you are an alien and stranger on the earth. Have you forgotten this? Begin to critique your choices. Most of us do not pay attention to the potential effect our daily choices have on our souls. Every day for the next 50 days, complete the following two statements:

A good choice I made recently was . . .
A foolish choice I made recently was . . .

Learning to make soul-conscious choices helps you be more than a survivor as you travel your life-path through the world. It gives you the power to thrive spiritually.

Let's go back to Moses for a moment. Over the years, he sees that a foolish choice he made was to take action for himself and murder the Egyptian. He sees that a good choice was to marry Zipporah and learn whatever he could about God from her father, Jethro the priest. And eventually, he makes the most soul-conscious choice of his life.

One day he finds it is not only his head burning and blazing under the hot desert sun; it is his heart as well, for he has seen a bush aflame with the fire of God. The God of the Hebrews, his God, has told him to go back to Egypt—something he would never do on his own, for through the years he has learned and grown accustomed to the lesson of *Gershom*, the reality of wandering as an alien in the land. Now God has, unmistakably, told him to go back and lead his people (who wouldn't accept him) out of slavery. Moses makes a decision.

Perhaps he remembers, *A good choice I made was . . . to learn whatever I could about God. A foolish choice I made was . . . to take action for myself.* Then the answer becomes clear: Don't go your own way, Moses. Go the way of God. *Go the way of God; go with God, go with God.* The words echo in his head as Moses follows the choice that will grow his soul to heights beyond what most of us can dream.

Reality Checkpoints

The Oath of Citizenship, which immigrants pronounce upon becoming citizens of the United States, reads in part,

> I hereby declare, on oath, that I absolutely and entirely renounce and abjure all allegiance and fidelity to any foreign prince, potentate, state, or sovereignty of whom or which I have heretofore been a subject or citizen; that I will support and defend the Constitution and laws of the United States of America against all enemies, foreign and domestic; that I will bear true faith and allegiance to the same.[2]

As a reality check, let's imagine some sort of heavenly immigration official has been watching the way you live your life. His role is to examine whether or not you are a fraud. Just by watching you, the way you behave, the actions that show what you really believe, what oath of allegiance will he determine you have taken? To what citizenship will this tough observer say you have given your fidelity?

I hope you, like the wonder-working wanderer, will allow God to test you in the wilderness of life. I hope you will resolve to turn your back on the Egypt of your past and move toward the hard-won Promised Land. I hope your soul—through the burning, bleaching, and blazing of those difficult life-choices—grows to flourish as an alien in a foreign land.

CHAPTER 2

Joseph: The Displaced Person of Integrity

THEME
Flee All-Too-Convenient Evil

TEXT
Genesis 39:1–23

APPLICATION 2
Agree to Flee

IN FLANNERY O'CONNOR'S short story "The Displaced Person," Mrs. Shortley, along with her shiftless husband, Chancey, serves as hired help on a 50-acre farm owned by the widow Mrs. McIntyre. A Pole, escaping the camps and the conflagration of World War II in Europe, has been resettled with his family as paid workers on the farm. Speaking of them, Mrs. Shortley defines a displaced person to the Black workers, Astor and Sulk.

> "They ain't where they belong to be at," she said. "They belong to be back over yonder where everything is still like they been used to. Over here it's more advanced than where they come from. But yawl better look out now," she said and nodded her head. "There's about ten million billion more just like them . . ."

This veiled threat is meant to indicate that if the Negroes didn't shape up, they could be replaced. It's not too long before the Shortleys discover it is they themselves who can be replaced.

This veiled threat is one that Mrs. McIntyre also uses regarding Mrs. Shortley's help, and thereby the ironies of displacement are set rolling by Flannery O'Connor, a shrewd observer of redemption as it shoves against the human condition. Who really is the displaced person? The story poses that we are all displaced, displaced by our prejudice and ignorance and indolence and blind-sightedness; displaced by our selfishness and fear of the unknown and our hatred of change.

At first, Mrs. McIntyre crows over the utility of her new foreign worker, Mr. Guizac. He can do everything. He's a hard worker, full of initiative; he's an excellent mechanic. She buys new farm equipment her unskilled labor couldn't possibly manage, but she now has hired help who possesses operating know-how. "That man there . . . he has to work! He wants to work!" she says, turning to Mrs. Shortley. "That man is my salvation!" On the farm, things are accomplished that Mrs. McIntyre thought never would be completed.

Of course, the boss woman's favor turns the other farm workers against the Displaced Person. Subtly, and not so subtly, they begin to undermine his position by using the very threat of displacement ("millions of billions waiting to take your place") against the farm's owner.

> She had noticed . . . that the Pole and all his family were getting fat; she pointed out to Mr. Shortley that the hollows had come out of their cheeks and that they saved every cent they made. "Yes'm, and one of these days he'll be able to buy and sell you out," Mr. Shortley had ventured to say, and he could tell that the statement had shaken her.

Mrs. MacIntyre informs the Catholic priest who had arranged for the Polish family to live and work on the farm that she's planning to fire the displaced person: "He's extra and he's upset the balance around here . . . and I'm a logical practical woman and there are no ovens here and no camps and no Christ Our Lord and when he leaves, he'll make more money. He'll work at the mill and buy a car and don't talk to me—all they want is a car."

O'Connor's "The Displaced Person" is a study of how, to our own damnation, we hate the stranger in our midst. In one unpremeditated moment, the Negroes and Mr. Shortley and Mrs. McIntyre conspire without words, their hatred in alliance, and allow a preventable tractor accident. Slipping its gear, which Mr. Shortley has deliberately set carelessly, the rolling machine crushes the unwarned Mr. Guizac, breaking his back. This kind of evil, the writer hints, is potentially present in all of our hearts.[1]

After World War II ended in 1945, much of Europe housed refugees displaced from war zones and from destroyed cities and villages. Most of these refugees attempted to resettle back at their residences of origin after the armistice. However, the Jewish population in particular—those who survived the death camps—had no place to go. In some cases, such as with Polish Jews, they were not welcome. Brigands killed or intimidated those who were unprotected; former communities no longer existed; possessions had been scattered. There was nothing

to go home to. So transit camps were hastily con-
structed, some close to the infamous concentration
camps that had been the scene of the destruction of
millions of their fellows, while the international community argued the plight of these displaced persons.
Understandably, correspondents and resettlement
officials discovered that most of these traumatized
people refused to think of anywhere on the European
continent, apart from France, as their home.

President Harry Truman lobbied Congress hard
to absorb as many refugees as public opinion and the
law would allow, but these proved to be formidable
obstacles. Despite the international publicity regarding the plight of European Jewish refugees, despite
disbelief at the inhuman genocide perpetrated by the
Nazi regime, despite shock and outrage, a Gallop
poll published in December 1945, indicated that 37
percent of the respondents agreed that they wanted
fewer European immigrants allowed into the United
States than had been allowed before the war, while
32 percent said they would settle for the same number but no more. Only 5 percent wanted an increase,
and 14 percent said they wanted no immigrants from
Europe at all.

Why this xenophobia, this distrust of the
stranger? Well, the stranger all too frequently con-
fronts us with situations we prefer not to examine.
And sometimes that confrontation has to do with the
condition of our own souls. We Christians are aliens
and strangers on the earth, Scripture reminds us. The

apostle Peter made plain that our role as displaced people—held in this transit camp earth, looking for our heavenly homeland—is to "declare the praises of him who called you out of darkness into his wonderful light" (1 Peter 2:9). To those who are still in darkness, who prefer the shadows, this declaration may be considered an affront.

A Character Hero

I often wonder, when I read the story of Joseph in Genesis, how much the universal latent fear of the displaced person shaped the tale. Certainly, the envy and jealousy of the older brothers toward this late-born son of the other wife, both favored by their aging father, Israel, caused them to commit an unspeakable act of near fratricide, which they would regret the rest of their lives. Joseph is sold (as good as dead) to a Midianite merchant and ends up on brutal slave blocks in cosmopolitan Egypt.

He is bought by Potiphar, Pharaoh's captain of the guard. Scripture tells us,

> The Lord was with Joseph, and he prospered. . . . Potiphar put him in charge of his household, and he entrusted to his care everything he owned. . . . The Lord blessed the household of the Egyptian because of Joseph. The blessing of the Lord was upon everything Potiphar had, both in the house and in the field. (Genesis 39:2–5)

Joseph is a displaced person, abandoned and betrayed and without a homeland; he "ain't where [he] belong to be at." What amazes me about this history is how unerringly straight the internal compass of Joseph's personal integrity stays pointed. The very vagaries of displacement allow us to create for ourselves the identity we choose to create. When we land in a place we do not belong, no family or friends or parental colleagues can insist that we behave. No external moral authority imposes itself upon us. We must live out of the center of what we determine is our most essential self. When we become displaced, most of us don't have an internal compass strong enough to keep us from wickedness, profligacy, laziness, arrogance due to our own successes, or the misuse of power when control falls into our hands.

François Fenelon, writing in *Christian Perfection,* speaks of the hazards of ill hidden within that shake themselves loose during the moments of displacement in our human journeys. He writes,

> Each of us carries in the depth of his heart a mass of filth, which would make us die of shame if God should show us all its poison and horror. . . . I am not speaking now of those whose hearts are gangrenous with enormous vices. I am speaking of the souls which seem honest and pure. We should see a foolish vanity which does not dare to come out in the open, and which stays in shame in the

deepest folds of the heart. We should see self-complacency, heights of pride, subtle selfishness, and a thousand windings within, which are as real as they are inexplicable. We only see them as God makes them emerge.[2]

In the lands of displacement, alert Christians begin to detect qualities about themselves they have not noticed at home, where all is comfortable, familiar, where the societal moray eels maintain order. Such a person sees she is selfish, pushing others away in the bread line. He exalts himself, telling little stories to puff his ego; she drops names of important people she has known and exotic places she has visited, attempting pathetically to raise her own esteem among other strangers. He whines and complains; she casts a wanton glance. They collaborate with the enemy.

Most of us forget what the true design of the enemy of our souls is: His desire is to utterly destroy us. Evil is evil even when it comes wrapped in attractive packages. Richard Crossman, a former editor of the *New Statesman and Nation,* and an Oxford professor, visited Dauchau with British intelligence shortly after the concentration camp was liberated. His account is a terrible but true analogy of the insensitivity to sin that is hidden within the heart of us all.

As we entered the camp we turned left to see the crematorium. We passed a long line of bullock carts—with sullen peasants standing by. The carts were laden with corpses taken from the crematorium. . . .

Just at the crematorium there were half a dozen camp inmates sitting in the shade of a pine tree, nonchalantly watching the corpses being arranged with pitchforks on the carts. Obviously they were immune to any sense of horror at the sight, and even their sense of smell apparently had been deadened.[3]

Accounts like these, not just about the World War II Nazi death camps but about all the incidents of unrestrained evil throughout time, are hideous pictures of the true intent of our enemy. His design is to destroy us physically, emotionally, psychologically, spiritually. He wants to order a death camp in our lives. So when he dangles an enticing bauble, let us flee. Let us remember the metaphors of horror that history has supplied and rip from our souls those evils we nurture and cherish that will lead to our destruction.

Joseph's inner compass was fixed upon integrity. No wonder theologians consider him a prefiguration of the Christ who was to come!

Mrs. MacIntyre, as she argues with the priest about sending away her hired-hand displaced person, angrily blurts out, "As far as I'm concerned, Christ was just another D.P." Joseph foreshadowed Christ, and conversely, we can view Jesus through this lens of displacement: "He was in the world, and though the world was made through him, the world did not recognize him. He came to that which was his own, but his own did not receive him" (John 1:10–11).

Sometimes while dealing with a displaced person in our midst who throws all our perceptions and systems out of whack, we just want to cut the intruder down to size. When challenged by Christ's perfect and powerful authority, the authorities of Israel, both religious and secular, used human authority to end his life by crucifixion, thinking, "We sure cut that upstart down to size. He really didn't belong here anyway."

When faced with the temptation to sexual pleasure exacted by the insistent wife of his master, Joseph's compass stays fixed. He says to her, "How . . . could I do such a wicked thing and sin against God?" Potiphar's wife persists, but "though she spoke to Joseph day after day, he refused to go to bed with her or even be with her" (Genesis 39:9–10). Joseph's compass stays fixed because he recognizes that the success he has experienced is due to the blessing of God; God's hand is upon him and God's presence is with him. Any sin will be a transgression against this reality and will surely result in loss. And Joseph knows that if he loses that interior homeland, he will have wasted his meaning for existence.

Day after day she spoke to the young man. Was there no other servant in the household who realized what was going on? Had any given in to the temptation to be her lover and did anyone know Joseph was her latest fixation? Or were they all jealous of this perfect overseer? Did they hope a noose was knotting around his neck? Had their sloth and distemper been shown up by his work ethic and evenness? Were many of them thinking in their hearts, "He's extra and he's upset the balance"? And is that why no one came forth to defend the Semite outsider, to state to the wrathful slaveholder, "Potiphar, master, have you any idea what has been going on around here?"

Did Potiphar not have a husband's instinct that his wife was obsessively attracted to the dark and handsome youth? Or was there something ill in his soul—despite the unusual blessings in house and field since Joseph had taken charge—that hated to be bettered by a foreigner, someone he himself had lodged in his own dwellings?

In her vengeful lie after Joseph has fled, leaving his garment behind in her hand, Potiphar's wife seems to employ that stratagem, the innate distrust of the stranger. "That Hebrew slave you brought us came to me to make sport of me." (He's extra; he's upset the balance around here.)

Joseph's amazing story is proof of this spiritual truth: *God is with those alert aliens who flee all-too-convenient evil*. Unlike many displaced persons, the temptations that surrounded Joseph were the temptations of excess. He was plummeted from the poverty of slavery into the lavishness of economic fortune.

Perhaps you've heard the story of the young woman who came to the United States to study theology. Upon entering a U.S. supermarket for the first time, she fainted. She was used to empty shelves and day-long lines for food, and her senses simply failed her when she observed the bewildering extravagance on the jammed shelves of an American superstore.

Joseph's unerring instinct protected him from the temptations of success. He remembered that the blessings on his life came from the hand of God; he was alert enough to exercise humility. He saw that he was a steward who served human masters who had chosen him to oversee their estates; he understood to whom the things he managed belonged. He remembered that if he gave in to the temptations available on every side, he could lose the blessing and the promise that was his future. He was alert to the truth that sexual purity was an instant measurement of the depth of his commitment to personal integrity. So he fled the all-too-convenient evil that was at hand.

Application Step: Agree to Flee

Whether you know it or not, as a Christian in our culture, you are a displaced person. The morals and values determined by adhering to the system of absolute truths outlined in Scripture put you instantly at odds with the world, particularly this oversexed, morally challenged, materially dominated society. As Mrs. Shortley would profoundly say, "You ain't where you belong to be at." Please, don't ever forget this. You do not want comfort to be your primary goal in life. Pleasure-seeking should not be your singular passion. A fat investment portfolio is not your ultimate gain.

You do not want to give in to sin that will lead you into a collaboration with the enemy. And since sexual opportunities and addictions—as well as many other sins—are so prominent in our culture, we have devised an acronym that might help you to act like Joseph when, day after day, temptation insists that you "lie" with it. The acronym spells out FLEE. The steps are as follows:

Feel the danger. Often we don't even realize when we're being tempted. We don't sense the danger lurking behind that TV commercial or that sexy billboard as we gaze at it. The daily bombardment of sexual messages tends to desensitize us to the inherent pitfalls. The prospect of sinning in private, without the shame of any public identification, offers tantalizing possibilities to those who are susceptible. Pornography on the Internet and X-rated movies in the video store, not to mention the sexual sewage available through cable channels, has made illicit sexual material handy, to be peered at behind closed doors in our own homes. Private rooms and private minds can hide our anger or judgmental thoughts, our hatred, materialism, or gluttony. Resolve right now to arrest the process of seduction by replacing the spiritual batteries in your temptation alarm. *Sound the soul alert* the moment you recognize temptation for what it is, and then . . .

Leave the area. Turn off the TV or close down the computer. Put down the magazine. Tear out the offending pages and throw them away. Walk away from a situation to get a new perspective. Make a decided effort to change not only your external environment but also your internal mindset, especially if leaving isn't possible. Ask God to help you take a mental detour by refocusing your mind on positive, healthy thoughts.

Experience God's pleasure. Hurray! You fled that all-too-convenient evil and pleased your heavenly Father! Even though you may or may not have sensed God's pleasure immediately, ask yourself what he would say to you if you could hear him at this moment. What would you say to a child or a friend who did what you just did? Speak those words out loud to yourself. Put your name in that phrase of commendation. When you make fleeing all-too-convenient evil a habit, over the long haul you will experience much greater satisfaction by delighting in living by the rules of heaven than by collaborating with the soul-destructive techniques of the enemy.

Establish protections. What can you do to shield yourself from such temptation in the future? Could you change your route to work so you won't drive by that adult book store? Maybe buy software that prevents offensive websites? Try finding a quiet, secluded corner in which you can avoid the locker room gossip. Block the shopping channel, or cancel your membership in the romance fiction book club.

Set up rules for your behavior so you won't even come close to yielding. Weed out all chances for compromising situations. When possible, evade the source of temptation. If you're experiencing an especially tough time in this area, it's important that you find a friend who will hold you accountable, or seek out a professional counselor, or join a prayer group and request intercessions for your weakness.

When our ministry began a religious television show, "You Need to Know," my husband David and I bought a television set. Then I remembered why we had raised our children without one. I am one of those persons who is susceptible to spending time in front of a television set. Subtly, perversely, I began to spend more and more evenings using the remote to flip channels. The television room was on the way to my bedroom; on my way to bed, I would pause "just to see what's on." It took a little while, but with the Holy Spirit's nagging conviction, we moved the television set to the basement, deliberately not connecting the antenna so we could only watch videos. The VCR now has a padlock on a little homemade lock box—thanks to the efforts of one of my sons—so that it takes a real act of intention to get the key, unlock the padlock, hook up the two plugs, and put in a video.

How can an intelligent women develop a viewing addiction? I can give you a thousand rationalizations, but the simple truth is, I—a woman who loves stories—am susceptible. I need to FLEE all-too-convenient evil.

We recommend that in order to be ready to FLEE temptation, you practice some flight simulations. Walk through the potential upcoming temptation. What will you say? Write some phrases down on a piece of paper. How will you exit the dangerous encounter? What kinds of excuses can you give to escape the grasp of the tempter (or temptress, or tempting object)? As much as you are able, go through the physical acts that will deliver you from the seduction to sin before it occurs. Practice turning off your computer. Write out a declaration of freedom and burn the catalogues that intrigue you. Build a little lock box; give the key to a friend. Throw the leftover pie in the garbage.

Joseph's secret can be yours: God is with those alert aliens who flee all-too-convenient evil.

Reality Checkpoints

Whenever citizens return to the United States after traveling overseas, they are given a U.S. Immigration form to fill out. One question always asks: Do you have anything to declare? A good test of soul alertness is how diligently we search ourselves to see if there is anything we need to declare about the condition of our souls. Self-examination, repentance, and confession are the hallmarks of spiritual maturity.

So, do you have anything to declare?

One pastor recently explained to a group who were eager to grow spiritually, "It is as though there is a long rope that connects our soul to God. When we sin, the rope is cut and we are disconnected. When we repent and confess, the rope is knotted and it is a little shorter. When we sin again, the rope is cut again. When we repent and confess, the rope is knotted, and it is a little shorter. Throughout our lifetime, though sin disrupts our relationship with our heavenly Father, the great gifts of repentance and confession draw us closer and closer to the heart of God."

Surely Joseph, in his arduous climb up through the ranks of slavery to the top of Potiphar's household, learned to declare each fall, each temptation, to his God. From this frequent confession, this daily "running home" to his heavenly Father, this model displaced person gained strength to flee from the all-too-convenient evil that assaulted him.

Similarly, you and I can declare to this world, "I ain't where I belong to be at." And when we've done so, we can run with all our strength away from the evil that threatens us and into the open heart of our Father.

CHAPTER 3

Esther: The Expatriate Who Preserved Her People

THEME
Rally Support to Shine for God

TEXT
Esther 4:1–16

APPLICATION # 3
Find Alien Allies

WHEN IT IS time to speak against great evil, one lone voice is like a sigh in the wind, but a chorus of voices rumbles like the waves on a beach or thunder over the mountains. The book of Esther is a study in communal strength when the exiled Jews, scattered through 127 provinces of the Persian Empire, faced imminent massacre.

Mordecai, cousin and adoptive father to Queen Esther, warns the young woman, "Do not think that because you are in the king's house you alone of all the Jews will escape. For if you remain silent at this time, relief and deliverance for the Jews will rise from another place, but you and your father's family will perish" (Esther 4:13–14). King Xerxes, potentate over the vast empire stretching from Ethiopia to India, has been manipulated by his vizier, Haman, to issue an anti-Semitic decree ordering the slaughter of all the Jews, beginning in the capital city of Susa.

The book of Esther is a perfect tale. It contains the glory and grandeur of an exotic locale, the ancient site of modern Iran. It stars some remarkable protagonists—a shrewd, righteous hero in Mordecai; a beautiful, intelligent, courageous heroine in Esther. The story is highly dramatic, with the power politics of the eastern court of King Xerxes and the heightened conflict of looming genocide for the Jews. And it sports a villain worthy of our hatred, Haman, whose evil intrigue is foiled at the very last moment. At the end, most satisfactorily, everyone receives his or her just reward. The good are saved and elevated; the evil are revealed and destroyed.

One of the intriguing aspects in this biblical story is not the profile of courage it contains, but the handbook it unfolds on surviving the hazards of being expatriates in a hostile land. In the book of Esther, the Jewish foreigners band together to preserve their identity and lineage as a unique people who, though exiles in a strange land, are still governed by a divine theocracy.

An eunuch sent from the queen comes to Mordecai to question why he is wearing sackcloth and ashes at the king's gate. Through this messenger, Mordecai sounds the alarm to Esther, who is cloistered in the harem. He tells her about imminent danger to their fellow aliens. He establishes a radical strategy: She must see the king, despite the hazard to her life. (Those who dared approach the king without being summoned risked execution.)

Esther calls on the spiritual support of the entire Jewish community exiled throughout the empire; the people must plead to heaven and fast from food and drink for three days. Esther devises a plan that she senses might please her royal consort. Certainly it will give her time to sound out the ultimate question: Is she still favored? She extends an invitation to dinner (actually, two dinners—and oh, by the way, bring your top advisor with you) before she is confident enough in the king's love to reveal the insidious intrigue Haman is plotting. Meanwhile, behind the scenes (actually unnamed in this book), God joins forces with the efforts of the many. Mordecai is rewarded for uncovering a plot of regicide, and Haman is humiliated.

Esther reveals that not only has this scoundrel prepared a gallows for her cousin, but that he has instigated an edict putting her life at risk and forcing her to witness the annihilation of her people. Haman's fate is sealed. He is hanged on the very gallows he had prepared for Mordecai. Another edict is immediately sent through the land, countermanding the first and giving the Jews permission to band together and protect themselves from enemies. Even the house of Haman is delivered to Esther, who turns it over to Mordecai. King Xerxes honors Mordecai and elevates him to chief satrap, second only to the king.

Mordecai without Esther or Esther without Mordecai or either of them without Jewish solidarity, or any of them without the divine hand of God orchestrating an uncanny series of events and circumstances, would have been the makings of disaster. If we are going to be survivors as God's aliens and strangers in the world, if we are going to thrive as a Christian people under a spiritual theocracy, we must rally soul-support so we can shine wherever our Divine Regent positions us.

One phrase at the end of this story delights my soul, because it is the result of unusual communal solidarity. After the evil has been revealed and the second edict has been hastily published through the land, and after the Jews have defended themselves in the capital city as well as in the far-flung provinces of Persia, the Scripture reads, "For the Jews it was a time of happiness and joy, gladness and honor" (Esther 8:16).

In fact, the feast of Purim is still traditionally celebrated on the thirteenth through fifteenth days of the month of Adar. According to the Jewish calendar, these were the original dates for Haman's intended slaughter. At this time even today, the book of Esther is read and the congregation in the synagogue shouts and hisses whenever the name of Haman is mentioned. Purim is a joyful feast that commemorates deliverance.

The church needs realistic, practical models of aliens who rally soul-support to shine where God positions them, just as Esther did with her compatriot Jewish people. How interesting it is that when we read the New Testament, those of us in western Christendom usually interpret it privately, in spite of the fact that most of the epistles are addressed corporately, to groups of believers. The first letter of Peter (out of which comes this week's theme verse, 1 Peter 2:9–12) is addressed "to God's elect, strangers in the world, scattered throughout Pontus, Galatia, Cappadocia, Asia and Bithynia" (1:1). The verses of distinction to us are addressed to a community as well: "But you are a chosen people" (not person), "a people belonging to God" (again, not a person belonging to God).

When God's chosen people learn to rally soul-support in order to shine where God positions them, they will know his blessing and his power. Their souls will be kept alert. They will become change agents in foreign territories, fighting together against all the destruction of body and soul and social order that poisons the earth.

Travel Wisdom

After my premiere journey to Europe, I was naturally eager to go back. Imagine my amazement when my daughter's father-in-law gave a gift to the four women in his family, as well as to the mothers of his two daughters-in-law—six of us in all—of a ten-day vacation in Paris. What wonderful generosity!

So one bright week in May, we landed in that beautiful city, made our way to the Right Bank, and settled ourselves in. At Hotel Loti, an older hotel, we were ideally situated—one half-block from the Place Vendome over which the Ritz Hotel reigns, one half-block in the other direction to Jardin des Tuilleries, that grand park with the two magnificent museums, Le Louvre and L'Orangerie. And beyond that, the Champs-Elysees stretches out toward l'Arc de Triomphe. Yes, we found ourselves parked in the perfect spot!

The Metro, which we mastered, carried us quickly underground to all the *arrondissements* (districts) in the central city, where we spent the mornings following walking tours out of Frommer's Guide, then sipping coffee and breaking brioches in sidewalk cafes. A brisk walk from our hotel through the Tuilleries took us to Pont Royal, which crossed the Seine. Beyond that was the Isle de la Citie, with Notre Dame and Ste. Chapelle, the flower markets, and then the Left Bank's Latin Quarter with its variety of charming restaurants and shops.

Interestingly, none of the anxiety I had experienced while journeying across Europe surfaced in Paris. Of course, that was easy to figure. I'd been to the City of Light one time before, my college French was a little less rusty, I stayed in the same place every night, no work was required of me—and, most importantly, I was not alone but enjoyed the delightful company of other people.

I discovered when we American women pooled our little bits of knowledge about France, the combined information made a satisfying whole—or whole enough, at any rate. The right word one woman couldn't remember, the other could. The amount of French francs equivalent to the U.S. dollar was determined by committee. What one had read in a magazine or guidebook was shared with everyone. Someone's friend back home had said to be sure to see the Picasso Museum in the Le Marais *arrandissement* and had written the name down on a piece of paper. Another friend had raved about ice cream at Berthillon—the best in the world, certainly; we sampled *melon* and *fraise de bois* and agreed. All six of us benefited from each friend's recommendations.

Those who were good at directions or mathematics or translation helped the others. Maitre d's were charmed by the charmers; bargains were hunted out by the shoppers; prices were negotiated by the negotiators. We reminded one another not to forget things (purses, passports, metro tickets, shopping bags, credit cards) and commiserated with one another's mistakes. By the end of ten days, we felt pretty confident negotiating Paris—as long as we had each other.

Perhaps in your own travels you have seen that in foreign territory, the smaller the group of nationals, the higher the tolerance they have for what normally divides them. At home their relationships might have been slightly cool, but some thousands of miles away, it seems natural to chat, enjoy one another, strike common concerns, develop interdependence, tell traveler's tales.

"Oh, you're from the States, are you?"

"Yes, where do you come from? Canada? Oh, we love Canada. We visit every summer."

People you might not speak to in your own country are instant friends in foreign territory. When you are in a strange land, people with common backgrounds most often revert to a higher loyalty and allegiance. Resettling in the same neighborhood in Chicago, two families—one Russian and one Bosnian—get along just fine. Aussies and Kiwis (Australians and New Zealanders) have a grand time together in a U.S. restaurant. Those from Honduras or El Salvador coalesce as Central Americans. There are many kinds of Jews—the Ashkenazi from Europe, the Sephardi from the Arab countries surrounding Palestine, as well as others—but when the issue of genocide is raised, all differences, though they be real and difficult, are abandoned and the many become one.

Perhaps the greatest of travesties in human immigration scenarios is when immigrants take advantage of their own people. The majority of fraud perpetrated is by one people against its own kind, stealing money, forging papers. This violates some universal code of brotherhood: We help our own. Most of us are dismayed when those who have successfully resettled in a new country don't aid their fellow countrymen who come later. But a parallel travesty exists when Christians do not achieve the strength they need to make this earthly transit by building functioning communities of faith. We need to know that we need each other.

Application Step: Find Alien Allies

Just as Esther understood the importance of rallying spiritual support in order to function in the crucial role God had assigned her, we as God's expatriates on earth must learn to be dependent upon one another. For most of us, we have to make this happen. As an application step, we suggest that you work to put together one event—an evening meal in your home, time after a church service, or some other creative happening—with others about whom you've thought, "I'd like to get to know them better!"

Make sure the conversation centers upon the concept of your journeys through the world as Christians. How are you doing being Christian aliens in your world? What ways are you employing to integrate Christian meaning into living? Where do you need improvement? This single event is just a start. What you want to find is a sustaining "alien ally" relationship. We need to put people in our lives for the long haul, people who will support us, pray with us, gently hold us accountable, be there for us when we need them. And they must expect the same commitment from us.

A *Chicago Tribune* article with the headline "Bag Ladies plan for their futures by enjoying today" caught my eye several years ago. It featured a group of women in Oregon who realized they could easily become bag ladies if they didn't make future financial and social arrangements. The vital statistics were self-evident. Women live longer than men. If there is a divorce, men are more likely to marry younger women. About 75 percent of older men are married, whereas only 35 percent of older women are.

At the time of one study mentioned in this article (1990), the average man's income in the over-65 age-group was $13,000. For women, that figure dropped to $7,500; for African-American women it was even lower—about $5,600. Moreover, women live longer with fewer retirement benefits and less financial planning experience, often after having received lower wages than men.

Calling themselves Bag Ladies of the World, several groups of women—ranging in age from a twenty-four-year-old mother of twins to a sixty-nine-year-old divorcee retired and getting by on Social Security and alimony payments—formed support groups.

These groups of women realized that financial security in the future was important. So they began to pool a small, but continually growing, savings account. "We may purchase property together, and we may live together," said one. "A lot of the details of what will happen aren't out of the bag yet. But one of the things we are going to need is cash resources."

The future aside, many of the Bag Ladies said that day-to-day emotional support from the others was their biggest reward. The sixty-nine-year-old divorcee has two sons who live some distance from her. "I have not felt lonely and I have not felt isolated at all," she is reported to have said. "What is that song from the Beatles? . . . 'I'll get by with a little help from my friends.'"[1]

When I read this, I began to pull together a number of friends who would be there for one another. I wanted women for the long haul: friends who would help each other if husbands died, friends to laugh and endure the aging process with, friends with comparable strengths and interests. All the women in my covenant group are involved in professional ministry; all travel, some are on church or parachurch staffs. All are readers, thinkers. Some teach spiritual formation courses in colleges, many are published writers in the religious market. Due to the current hunger for spiritual mentors, three of the women have become trained and certified spiritual directors. One is ordained.

For eight years now, we have met together once a month and without a great deal of energy expended (apart from the task of coordinating our calendars to see when most of us can meet the next month—which is no small chore). We have been there for one another during job reversals, the distresses of raising adult children, laments about the midlife process. We have shared excellent books and articles and ideas and enjoyed a few retreats—one just for play, no praying allowed!

Recently, however, we have begun to challenge one another to a broader effort. All of us have spent our lives ministering to other people; we believe this is a high calling. We are appalled by how many younger women and young couples have no older, spiritual, wise mothers or fathers or married couples to mentor them. After months of praying and discussion and planning, we have launched a (mostly) long-distance mentoring program to walk with people as personally as possible into deeper spiritual growth through the facilities of e-technologies: e-zines, e-mail, a daily meditation website (www.thissacredspace.org), and a bimonthly print newsletter *(God's Sacred Rhythms)*. Why should we have so much to give with so many hungry for spiritual guidance and not use the technologies to make our cumulative wisdom, experience, and knowledge available?

Hungry Souls (see page 133) is the ministry that has evolved out of our own need for one another and the long relationship that has developed over nearly a decade of meeting as a covenant group. We are a worthy example of this week's theme: Rally support to shine for God.

In his book *The Lexus and the Olive Tree,* Thomas Friedman makes an excellent attempt to help his readers understand globalization, a complicated and overwhelming modern reality. Every so often I find writers who illumine my thinking, and Friedman, the *New York Times* Pulitzer Prize–winning foreign affairs columnist, always makes me glad I've taken time to read his work. "We are now in the new international system of globalization," he declares, having made the point that the world is no longer what we knew it to be, particularly during the Cold War years.

Friedman then defines the dynamic ongoing process he calls *globalization:*

> It is the inexorable integration of markets, nation-states and technologies to a degree never witnessed before—in a way that is enabling individuals, corporations and nation-states to reach around the world farther, faster, deeper and cheaper than ever before, and in a way this is enabling the world to reach into individuals, corporations and nation-states farther, faster, deeper, cheaper than ever before.[2]

With this integration occurring on a worldwide scale, the possibilities for Christian ministry beyond our own narrow shores are immense. I have rallied alien allies to help me do more than survive. They are in place to help me thrive spiritually but also to rally support for a task that is bigger than I am. The ministry of Hungry Souls is our way of shining in the world. What is yours?

Reality Checkpoints

After a plane disembarks at an international airport, and particularly if several airliners land at the same time, the lines at the immigration check-in can get frustratingly slow. Of course, for returning passengers it feels like the longest part of the trip; after traveling so far, everyone is in agony to get home. Loved ones are waiting beyond the doors, friends have come to pick up the weary world travelers. But one question from the customs official inevitably speeds the process: "Are you traveling as a family unit?" Husband, wife, children, relatives advance to the immigration counter as a group, and one inspection of the head of family's passport, with maybe a cursory glance at the others, will clear the party through.

So the question for you right now is: "On this earth transit, as aliens and strangers, are you traveling as a family, as part of God's family?" Believe me, if you answer yes, if you take refuge in the prayers and action of your people as Esther did, it will make the crossing go much faster.

CHAPTER 4

Nehemiah:
The Border Guard Who
Built Holy Walls

Theme

Rebuild Sacred Walls That Protect

Text

Nehemiah 2:11–18; 13:15–22

Application

Resolve to Resoul

D R. LARRY WARD had the most amazing way of going through customs. And in a seven-week trip around the world, we saw him in action many times.

At the invitation of Food for the Hungry, an international relief and development organization, my assignment was to observe many of the refugee hotspots of the world with fresh eyes. Then I was to go home and write about what I saw.[1] During 49 days of travel with the company's executive director, Dr. Ward, and his wife, Lorraine, we crossed the borders of over a dozen countries.

Lorraine and I—and whatever relief workers happened to be accompanying us on that leg of the journey—would pile all of our luggage on one airport trolley and follow our peerless leader, who was invariably dressed in an official-looking black shirt with a Nehru stand-up collar, black trousers, and a peaked black Indian cap perched on his white hair. Shouting something in garbled English, Larry would clutch all our passports and some innocuous documents in one fist, wave them in the air, then march directly past the customs inspection with his entourage fast on his heels, pushing the piled luggage.

We were never stopped or questioned; not one suitcase was opened. No customs official motioned to an armed guard as we swept past. And though I have crossed many borders in the world, I have never seen anyone but Dr. Larry Ward use this bold approach. I still don't know why it worked. As far as I could tell, it was nothing but an enormous bluff.

I've learned many lessons while crossing borders. Some of these bear directly on this chapter's theme of rebuilding sacred walls that protect. The First Border Crossing Principle is: *Never take no for an answer* (at least on the first, second, third, and forth try). Ask in different ways; ask different officials. Someone somewhere may know exactly how to help you.

Through the years, our lives have been enriched by many internationals who have lived with us. One—a beautiful young Brazilian woman with perfect English—was in her first year of college, majoring in English and American literature. Every summer, David and I take a few friends to the Shakespeare Festival in Canada, which maintains one of the finest repertory theater companies in the world. Naturally, because of our guest's literary interests, we particularly wanted to share this rich experience with her.

Early one Fourth-of-July morning we crossed the bridge from Detroit, Michigan, into Windsor, Ontario, and there Canadian Immigrations stopped us, directing our car to the parking area. David and our young friend, Luciana, went inside the immigrations building along with the husband of the other couple who were with us. In a little while, David appeared again, and I heard a cry that only means this is a situation he can't handle. "Karen, we need your help in here." His certain frustrated tone of voice always cues me.

Because our houseguest didn't have her F-1 student visa (though she had asked about border crossing requirements at a U.S. consulate office) but had, rather, an ancillary document, Canadian immigrations would not permit her entry. We would have to go back to Detroit, find a consulate office, and see if we could acquire a temporary permission. On a holiday? How could we possibly do this and reach Stratford for the 2:00 matinee performance for which we had purchased tickets? The more those in our party tried to "solve" our impossible situation, the more adamant the immigrations officials became, the more frustrated they all grew.

But I have watched experts cross borders. I know that "No!" does not always mean no. The Second Border Crossing Principle I have learned is: *The more difficult the situation, the softer the tone of voice you should use.* And the Third follows quickly upon the Second: *The immigrations officials of any country are always wiser than you are; show them that you know this.* All three principles were needed at this moment.

"Will you please explain exactly where we have gone wrong here?" I asked. Believe me, this is a great question with which to begin negotiations in many sticky situations!

Apparently, our Brazilian friend had received instructions from the U.S. consulate office in Chicago;

she also should have called the Canadian consulate, as the requirements are not the same.

So I continued (in a very soft tone), "Well, we have obviously made a mistake. We have not followed the correct procedure, and we beg your pardon. This young woman from Brazil is taking her college degree in Chicago." She gave a bright smile, her black eyes glowing as though on cue. "She lives in our home and is majoring in literature. Every year, for 20 years, my husband and I have driven up to attend the Shakespeare Festival, which we love. Naturally, we want to treat our friend to this event. Now, it is Independence Day in the States, and all the civic offices will be closed. We would like to make the 2:00 matinee, and I'm wondering whether you can advise us about any other legitimate options."

In the atmosphere of soft-spoken discussion and abject humility, the immigrations officer did remember another way. We filled out forms, a supervisor signed the papers; it was all perfectly legal, and it only cost us $80.00 and, to our relief, a short amount of time.

The Last Principle of Border Crossing I have learned is this: *Borders often exist for our own good.* Despite the inconvenience of boundaries, living within and understanding the territorial rules of a nation, of human relationships, or of spiritual growth can, indeed, provide exactly the safe environment we need to flourish.

A Character Hero

Any church undergoing a building program understands the chronicle of the restoration of the walls of
Jerusalem, which were laid waste during the sack of
the city by Nebuchadnezzar's troops in 587 B.C.
Nehemiah's grand scheme reaches into builder arche-
types that deeply touch the emotions of any vision-
ary, be it an individual or a community of people.
The daring task. The impossible circumstances. The
limitation of finances and workers. The hostile enemies. The disaffection of the working crews. The
focused leader who rallies his people to accomplish
tremendous goals. The dream realized. No wonder
Nehemiah so touches those who face the daunting
task of a building project!

In ancient culture walls were important. Their
condition indicated the wealth and standing of a city-
state. Good walls kept out hostile invaders, hoards
of brigands; checkpoints and guardians at the gates
controlled who entered and who exited. Sturdy
walls, insurmountable and formidable, kept the people within safe. Such enclosures defined their identity as citizens and ensured sanctuary as they worked
and lived.

Nehemiah (another Jewish expatriate in the court
of Persia), the trusted cup bearer to King Artaxerxes,
petitions his majesty in great fear, "Why should my
face not look sad when the city where my fathers are
buried lies in ruins, and its gates have been destroyed

by fire? . . . If it pleases the king . . ." (Nehemiah 2:2–5). With that toehold, this amazing administrator proceeds to negotiate for time to make a survey trip back to his homeland, official documents ensuring safe passage, and a decree to secure the building materials he needs from the keeper of the king's forest. Not bad work for one interview!

In record time, 52 days, Nehemiah and his intrepid band of Israelites rebuild the wall of Jerusalem. What most students of the Old Testament don't realize is that he built two walls—one outside Jerusalem and one in the souls of its people. How intriguing to examine the corollary between the material and the spiritual!

Nehemiah's construction crew rebuilt the stone walls of the city. But something else needed to be rebuilt in the lives of the city's bedraggled citizenry who were left in the land attempting to recreate their destroyed culture. Inscribed at one time by the finger of God on tablets stored in the Ark of the Covenant, the Commandments also laid neglected and in ruin. Raising again the city walls of stone became tangible evidence for the more ephemeral work that needed to be accomplished in the spiritual lives of this fragile and frayed, worn-out excuse for a nation.

"Rise up and build," Nehemiah commands, and the volunteers strengthen their hands for the good work. Listen to the rhythm of these phrases that are repeated again and again in the third chapter: they "laid its beams and set its doors, its bolts, and its bars . . . they repaired . . . they repaired . . . they rebuilt . . .

they restored." In my imagination, I can hear this construction litany accompanied by the rhythm of the stone-chippers' chisels, the cadence of carpenter's hammers and mallets, the hum of saws and twirling augers, the blast of the forgers' bellows. "And the wall was joined together to half its height," reports the chronicler, "for the people had a mind to work."

The second wall Nehemiah finds he must restore is that of the Levitical covenant, the spiritual boundary set up to protect Israel and mark them as the people of God. The reading of the Law brings brokenness and repentance because the remnant of the nation has not observed God's commandments (Nehemiah 8).

During this remarkable Old Testament reconstruction period, the wall of the soul Nehemiah puts in place is the restoration of the Sabbath practice. Presbyterian minister Wayne Muller writes in *Sabbath: Finding Rest, Renewal, and Delight in Our Busy Lives*:

> The Jewish Sabbath became crucial when the Temple in Jerusalem was destroyed. . . . When the Jews were in exile, the Sabbath became their temple, their sanctuary in time. It traveled with them wherever they went, a movable feast, a holy of holies that faithfully accompanied them in adversity. The practice of Sabbath was a spiritual glue that held the people together. This is perhaps why the Sabbath commandment is the one most discussed and reiterated throughout the Torah.[2]

Modern western Christians need to re-institute this sacred discipline as well, with appropriate understanding. We have a spiritual wall that is being destroyed by the secularized living of our post-Christian era. Consequently, the enemy of our souls is raiding our spiritual city. The boundaries that keep hostile invaders from sacking our territory lie in ruins. The border crossing, with its checkpoints and border guards and immigration officials, has been overrun. Though we attend church (for too many of us, only when we feel like it), though we grab at daily devotions (maybe five minutes before we race off to work), though we register for Bible conferences and listen to Christian radio in the car and buy stacks of religious literature (but can't find time to do the things we learn), our souls are languishing. We feel spiritually dry, bereft. The joy of salvation is a distant memory.

As I mentioned before, I have crossed many borders in the world. In addition, I have journeyed back and forth across this spiritual checkpoint called Sabbath. Just as certain border principles assist us in physical crossings, so other important border principles assist us in spiritual crossings.

The First Sabbath Principle is this: *You will never be able to rebuild the wall of your soul until you restore your understanding of and participation in Sabbath practice.* God's design for the renewal of his dear children is woven into the very fabric of creation, into the Old Testament cycle of feasts and festivals, and into the Ten Commandments.

Muller writes, "In the book of Exodus, we read, 'In six days God made heaven and earth, and on the seventh day God rested, and was refreshed.' Here, the word 'refreshed,' *vaiynafesh*, literally means, *and God exhaled.*"³ It is as though all of creation, the work of the world, was one long inhale; but the seventh day was God's enormous sigh: *It is good.* The inhale is not complete without the exhale. Indeed, the body is sustained by inhaling and exhaling; the breath that gives us life, that cleanses our blood, is an unconscious rhythm of inhaling and exhaling. So in spiritual life. The exhale, Sabbath, is given us by God so that our souls can sigh with ease, can take their rest.

The ancient Jewish rabbis emphasized that God gave the gift of *menuha*, or blessing, in each Sabbath. Here is to be found everything busy souls long for: quiet, repose, serenity, tranquility, peace. Here we set ourselves aside so grace can meet us and, when it does, so we can notice it.

The Second Sabbath Principle is: *Observing the Sabbath is not an option. It is God's injunction.* Let me remind you of these words from the Decalogue. The Fourth Commandment states, "Remember the Sabbath day by keeping it holy. Six days you shall labor and do all your work, but the seventh day is a Sabbath to the Lord your God. On it you shall not do any work, neither you, nor your son or daughter, nor your manservant or maidservant, nor your animals, nor the alien within your gates" (Exodus 20:8–10).

Some would argue that the Sabbath is an Old Testament principle, not one for the New Testament covenant. I grant that we may have to dialogue about the meaning and consequent practice of the Sabbath principle as Christians in a post-modern society, but if we obliterate this standard, what about the other nine commandments? We might argue, for instance, that in this sexually liberated culture, with the media assaulting fidelity and monogamy on every side, it is impossible to hold to the standard of not committing adultery!

Having struggled personally to live within the Sabbath principle, having extensively researched the topic and written a book on it *(Making Sunday Special),* and having profoundly benefited by its amazing meaning, I would contend that those who would cancel Sabbath have never experienced it and, consequently, don't understand it.

In her book *Keeping the Sabbath Wholly*, Dr. Marva Dawn unfolds a theological treatise on the need for moderns to recapture the Sabbath practice:

> To return to Sabbath keeping is not nostalgia or an attempt to return to an age that is pre-Enlightenment, pre-Industrial Revolution, and pre-Darwinian. Rather, it is a return to the spiritual dimension that haunts us. In an age that has lost its soul, Sabbath keeping offers the possibility of gaining it back. In an age desperately searching for meaning, Sabbath keeping offers a

new hope. In contrast to the technological society, in which the sole criterion of value is the measurement of efficiency, those who keep the Sabbath find their criteria in the character of God, in whose image they celebrate life.[4]

Here is a concept that may be new to you: *Observing the Sabbath is more than just going to church; it is a whole different approach to living out the week—week after week, year after year.* This is the Third Sabbath Principle. God asks us to give to him at least 24 hours each week. This is so far from the common practice of most Christians in contemporary society that it boggles the mind to think how razed this protective wall has become. Keeping the Sabbath holy is much, much more than going to church on Sunday mornings (or, for some, to church or synagogue on Saturday). It is learning to live within the week's sacred rhythm, which God designed for our own good.

In the Old and New Testaments, each new day began at sundown. So, for the practicing Jew, Sabbath begins on Friday evening and continues for 24 (actually 26) hours until Saturday evening at sundown. The day is so rich and rewarding, Jews begin to anticipate it and plan for it on Wednesday or Thursday; it is so meaningful, they carry the warmth and joy of it through Sunday, Monday, and Tuesday, when the cycle begins anew. This sacred rhythm enfolds the entire week—week after week—and cre-

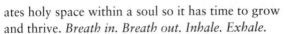

ates holy space within a soul so it has time to grow
and thrive. *Breath in. Breath out. Inhale. Exhale.*

This is the process of resouling that everyone who
practices Sabbath experiences. It is the reason God
gave us this great gift. "And so, only in the soil of
Sabbath tranquility can we seed the possibility of
beginning a new day, a new week—even a new life—
again and again, each time with fresh eyes, rested
and refreshed, born within the completely gratuitous
sanctuary of time."[5] Sabbath is the border that keeps
us safe, keeps intruders out, reminds us who we are
and helps us to remain whole and holy.

The final Sabbath Principle (and there are countless others) is: *Sabbath is a joyful gift given by a loving Creator so that sacred feasts and holy festivals
will not desist from his community of children.* If
your concept of Sunday is a day so bleak that you
actually dread it, if you have abandoned the Sabbath
altogether because of the undue strictures of a legal-
istic past, I have good news. That was not God's idea
for his day. It may have been the idea of a phari-
saical, bean-counting, religious legalist, but it is the
wrong idea. It certainly was a concept that infuriated
Jesus, and after all, he is Lord of the Sabbath. I can
just see him, in my mind's eye, hitting his forehead
in frustration with the open palm of a hand and saying, clearly, "Well, duh! Sabbath was made for man,
not man for the Sabbath."

One Jewish rabbi suggests we correct this miscon-
ception (or tear down and rebuild the ugly architectural

disaster of a wall) by simply saying, "Today I am going to pamper my soul." In other words, ask yourself, "What can I do in these 24 hours to help recreate my true self? What will cause me to resoul?"

Let me emphasize that Sabbath understanding is so broad and profound—and Sabbath practice so all-embracing in its revolutionary effect on how we think, act, and live—that these four Sabbath principles are only the entryway into a life-changing spiritual discipline with the potential to utterly shatter the creeping, grasping, entangling tentacles of encroaching secularism.

If you, a spiritual alien and stranger on the earth, want to do more than survive in this culture in which you live, if you want to thrive spiritually, you must learn to rebuild sacred walls that protect. And one of these walls is a boundary in time, the Sabbath.

Application Step: Resolve to Resoul

Consider how you can build a wall around some part of your weekend to protect Sabbath space for yourself and for God. Maybe you have developed a Sabbath discipline, and this exercise will help you to refresh it. Perhaps you have no Sabbath practice or understanding; this will help you begin. Ask yourself two questions: What kind of activity (or nonactivity) tends to recharge my spiritual and emotional batteries? What day or part of my weekend will I build a wall around so I can resoul?

Being intentional is a way to stay in touch with the condition of our own inner selves, the part of us that responds to holiness. The Sabbath practice, as much as any other discipline I know, will bring renewal to your mind, body, and soul. It is God's great gift to his people, and leaving it neglected, as one writer has said, is like not opening the biggest present under the Christmas tree.

Build a wall around some part of your weekend experience so that your soul will have space and time and quiet and joy enough to flourish.

Reality Checkpoints

The headlines of a *Time Magazine* Special Issue read: "Welcome to America," and the blurb on the cover stated, "The border is vanishing before our eyes, creating a new world for all of us." The issue featured articles examining the effects of the vanishing border between the U.S. and Mexico—and, of course, this is only part of a much larger globalization that is changing the way we view ourselves and function in the world. Some analysts project that due to the "democratization of technology, of finance and of information" there will be no borders as we have known them, the ultimate result of globalization.

For the Christian alien on the earth, however, borders will always be important. The wall of our inner city is the way we retain our unique identity and remind ourselves of our non-resident status in the world.

Consider, therefore, these two questions: How are you different, in positive ways, from those around you who do not call themselves Christians? What borders have you determined you will not cross in order to maintain the essential distinction from the society that surrounds you?

This is where you step in, my friend. Allow your weekly rhythm to help you realize the dream of Nehemiah. Despite the seemingly impossible circumstances of a busy schedule, the hostile enemies of time and culture, the disaffection of those around you, you can dare to build the wall of Sabbath soul-rest, renewing yourself as one of God's chosen people.

CHAPTER 5

Paul: The Cross-Cultural Communicator

THEME
Reference the Culture to Share God's Love

TEXT
Acts 17:16–34

APPLICATION 5
Compliment the Culture

MY HUSBAND, David, was scheduled to meet with a coalition of Christian leaders in Denver, and when our plane arrived behind schedule, I told him to rush ahead so he would not be late. I would wait for the luggage, catch a taxi, check into the hotel, and come along when I could.

My taxi driver had a thick accent and was from one of the former Soviet bloc nations. Intrigued with the whole process of immigration and resettlement, I am always interested in what country foreigners are from and how they have landed here. This man and his family had settled in the Denver area a few years before.

"And how are you doing in the States?" I inquired.

"Oh, the United States!" he exclaimed, craning his neck while attempting to make eye contact with me in the back seat. "Here is wonderful. Here you can get job, feed family, have home. Here you do what you want, be anything. I love United States."

On and on he went, extolling the virtues of his adopted homeland the entire short journey from the airport. By the time I arrived at the hotel, my eyes were filling with tears. I, who am often critical about the failings of my own country—its materialism and militarism—was soundly reminded why I love this flawed but remarkable land. I heard once again how good this "new world" has been to so many people who long to achieve those basic liberties our founding fathers sought to ensure.

A Character Hero

I wonder what was the response of those Athenians confronted by Paul in the pages of Acts? Perhaps they, too, had almost forgotten one of the great things about their land. And yet the apostle brought one of the great characteristics of Athens back to their attention.

Obviously, Paul is disturbed by the innumerable idols he sees across the city. Acts 17:16 reports that "he was greatly distressed." As usual when Paul is present, the Jews in the synagogue and the God-fearing Greeks develop a dialogue that escalates into a lively exchange: "A group of Epicurean and Stoic philosophers began to dispute with him" (verse 18). He is invited to be part of the open forum discussion in the Areopagus, the place in Athens where ideas were formally exchanged.

But before he begins to speak, it appears from the text that he changes tactics. He begins by complimenting the culture. "Men of Athens! I see that in every way you are very religious. For as I walked around and looked carefully at your objects of worship, I even found an altar with this inscription: To an Unknown God" (verses 22–23).

What a communicator! Paul begins with a positive, than builds the message of the gospel out of the one thing he could find exemplary about the polytheistic worship of those Greeks—they were religious.

The Athenians may have felt something like I did when the foreign taxi driver lectured me on the greatness and generosity of my own country. I was certainly prone to be favorable to the messenger!

My husband and I have both journeyed in the far-flung reaches of the world, but rarely with each other. So when our fortieth wedding anniversary approached, we decided to allot a portion of some inheritance funds to visit many of the sites of the ancient civilizations of the Mediterranean. In ruin after ruin, we were impressed with how the apostles—common folk really, fishermen and tax collectors, trades people and tentmakers—challenged the pagan culture.

Along with the crowd one hot May morning, we climbed the stairs to the Acropolis that towers over the modern city of Athens. Even in ruins the Parthenon, devoted to the worship of the goddess Athena, is the highest building on the mount. "That's Mars Hill," said David, pointing to an outcropping below us. Mars Hill, one of the places at which Paul preached. The reality was stunning. This huge artifact behind us was still able to convey—without much manufactured imagination on my part—the grandeur and glory that was ancient Greece. There in my mind's eye was the apostle, fearlessly, relentlessly, cleverly translating the transforming power of the living Christ. He was only a Jew from some little backwater nation called Israel, yet he confounded these urbane, educated, and advanced intellectuals of Athens. Paul was a genius at referencing the culture to share Christ's love.

While wandering through the excavations of Ephesus—a sprawling, miles-long-and-miles-wide archeological dig—we could easily conclude that the city had once been a sophisticated center of culture and commerce, economics and trade. I was overwhelmed with how fearlessly Paul dialogued with the Ephesians. "Paul entered the synagogue and spoke boldly there for three months, arguing persuasively about the kingdom of God" (Acts 19:8).

What happened? Eventually, Paul and the disciples begin holding daily public discussions in the lecture hall of Tyrannus and, because Christianity always challenges pagan worship (and its economic underpinnings), a riot ensues, led by the silversmiths who make shrines of the goddess Artemis. Angered, the people gather into the theater. The ruins of the one I saw was said to hold 20,000, an estimated tenth of the population of Ephesus at that time. I thought about that open-air stadium, how its atmosphere was electrified and how Paul had to be restrained from charging into it, lest he be killed in the uproar (verse 30).

Instead of Paul, Gaius and Aristarchus, fellow disciples, appear before the mob. The city clerk quiets the confusion, saying, "You have brought these men here, though they have neither robbed temples nor blasphemed our goddess. . . . The courts are open and there are proconsuls. [You] can press charges" (verses 37–38), and he dismissed the mob. Obviously, though the apostles and the disciples are preaching the gospel, they had not violated the laws of the system that kept order in that great cosmopolitan city.

We moderns have many lessons to learn from the witnesses to Christ who have gone before us. Imagine how I would have felt if the Denver taxi driver had harangued about everything that was wrong with the States, if he had complained and whined and cursed the ground we were driving over. I might have been sympathetic to his distresses, but I wouldn't have liked him or his message. Historically, the mission of the church has always been advanced when missionaries of the gospel learned to affirm and identify with the culture.

Heads up. We are aliens and strangers on the way to a much better world. In the meantime, our mandate from God is to live in a way that brings light to the darkness, justice to corrupting systems, compassion and mercy to circumstances of uncompromising neglect and cruelty.

Let us begin this enormous task, which few Christians seem to accomplish well, by affirming what is good in our culture. In order to succeed, we are going to have to learn its language and then translate the meanings of Christianity into that language. What is the language of our culture? It is multifold: the language of business, the language of science, the language of government, the language of literature, the language of leisure and entertainment. . . .

For instance, I am fairly knowledgeable about the languages of film, literature, business, or horticulture. I try to build bridges between these areas of study to others who use similar lexicons. One of the great failings of the church is that it asks the broader culture to understand *its* language. This post-Christian culture has no working literacy in the Bible, nor does it comprehend such theological terms as "redeemed," "saved," "washed in the blood," or "sanctified." Do you wonder why you feel you are speaking a foreign language when you try to share the roots of faith? For most in our culture, you are unintelligible.

But I have good news for you. All the fields mentioned above have analogies, metaphors, and comparisons. These can lead to serious discussions of faith and values—and, eventually, Christian meaning. We who are followers of Christ, like Christ himself, can learn to reference the culture to share his love.

Application Step: Compliment the Culture

A challenging examination of the debate between belief and unbelief is the film *The Third Miracle*, starring Ed Harris as a priest whose faith has been shattered by doubt and Anne Heche as the skeptical adult daughter of a woman reported to have worked miracles. Set in the Catholic diocese of Chicago, the priest is an investigator of miracle claims. (The church seriously attempts to determine if fraud or frenzy underlie any outbreaks of bleeding statues, weeping Madonnas, healings, or other paranormal events.) In his role as an investigator of the church, the priest has lost his faith; there has been too much fraud and frenzy. *The Third Miracle* tells how this displaced believer finds his way back to faith, or at least to the early fragile flowerings of trusting God again.

This film describes well the existential spiritual state of many in our society. If we train ourselves to compliment our culture, some intriguing discussions will begin with the conversation gambit, "I saw a really interesting film the other night." In an exchange about *The Third Miracle*, I would intentionally draw out existing skepticism, anger over hypocrisy, or dismay with the institutional church: "You sound like something really bugs you about Christianity. Want to tell me about it?" Then I would just listen. It is amazing what healing is available for the spiritually disillusioned when Christians resist the temptation to argue and just shut their mouths and listen.

Several years ago I was lecturing in a Sunday evening service for a Mennonite Brethren church in Lancaster County, Pennsylvania. My topic was "Using Popular Culture to Tell God's Stories." I established a premise by which to analyze films—or television, or literature, or music—from a Christian worldview. We must be cautious if we are going to learn the languages of the cultures through which we are journeying as aliens and strangers. (Soul alert!

Soul alert!) If we are not careful, our souls can become fixated, addicted, smudged, soiled, distressed, and mutilated. Then, having no idea what kind of cultural literacy would be active in a church like this in Pennsylvania, I asked the audience to give examples of films that could stimulate faith or values dialogues with non-Christians, folk who might even be hostile to Christianity.

We experienced an evening so stimulating, so invigorating, so helpful and defining, it is a crying shame churches don't organize regular discussion nights for congregation members to teach one another how to exercise caution, draw out hidden or overt intentions in films, or reference the culture to tell of Christ's love.

A successful film and television producer and his wife have opened their home for just this sort of discussion among people from their church. Their plan for beginning was to choose films with intentional Christian meaning. Hard to do? Not as hard as you might think. The three films they chose for this test effort were: *Walking Across Egypt* with Jonathan Taylor Thomas and Ellen Burstyn, a movie which examines the effect of Christian love and hospitality on a delinquent teenager; *Monseigneur Quixote*, a marvelous rendition of the Graham Greene novel about a modern Spanish churchman in the modern guise of a Cervantes-like medieval tilter; and . . . *The Third Miracle*.

Together, as aliens and strangers—with a few people trained in critical analysis or an available literature professor from a nearby college or some young folk who have really studied film—we can begin to uncover the hidden and overlooked meanings of terrific, mediocre, and even terrible films. As one Christian analyst said to me, "Even bad films can be used for the sake of the gospel."

Paul complimented the culture. He found what he could affirm: "Men of Athens! I see that in every way you are very religious." The taxi driver said, "Oh, the United States! Here you can eat. You can feed family." We need to carefully learn to do the same. The untapped potential in this approach may win a hearing for the gospel beyond anything we might have dreamed possible.

Some rules of thumb have helped me compliment the culture for the sake of opening discussions about faith and values. *First, if a film or book or television show has a wide following, I attempt to see or read it in order to be informed.* This comes with discretion. After reading part of one Anne Rice novel, it was so darkly evil, I tossed it into the garbage, thus exercising my privilege of active judgment. Obviously, I can not and will not be exposed to everything, so these are dips into culture to keep me somewhat current, although I find that waiting a year or two or three doesn't hurt. Many people I want to talk with wait a year or two or three as well. We all lead busy lives.

I always apply a Christian analytical premise to my reading or viewing. What is the worldview of the creators behind this piece of work? Is it Christian? Is it anti-Christian? What, if any, is its moral message? Would Christ view this? What would he say about it? What do I agree with? What do I reject?

I also attempt to establish dialogue with careful thinkers who are Christian. Having seen an Academy Award–winning film I would not go into a theater to view (I am in control of the remote at home and can fast-forward or turn off objectionable scenes), I was nevertheless moved by the portrayal of an American middle-class family who were lost in the most spiritual sense of that word. My friend, however, a Hollywood producer who considered the same film well-made and had studied it closely for professional reasons, concluded that it was "a dangerous film" and pointed out elements I had not seen in my one-time observation. I just wish I'd been in a dialogue with non-Christians as well when our engaging conversation was unfolding.

What I'd like you to do for the application step this week is to find ways to compliment the culture. What have you said that's good about the president, the prime minister, the government? Conduct a conversation with several friends about a newspaper article that conveyed moral impact to you. Join a book group and read what others are reading; listen to their conversation as an active tutorial on secular thinking. Take a popular business book and see if you can discover principles that are value-laden with Judeo-Christian roots; then talk about it over coffee break with your colleagues. Read an ethical discussion on

genetics, for instance, and see what Christian impli-
cations this has on your view of God as Creator. Ask
questions of a biochemist as a discussion starter. You
don't have to be brilliant to ask questions, but if you
ask good ones, people will think you are!

Become an intentional hunter of metaphors,
analogies, illustrations to springboard useful conversation. Probably your most valuable resource will be
other Christians who are culturally exposed, who see
Christian meaning in professional systems and who
are wrestling daily with the moral and ethical concerns of being faithful believers in the marketplace.

Become aware of how frequently you are judgmental of the world around you. Certainly, the world
is fallen and we know it is not our home. But does it
reflect in some ways the one who created it? Can you
be tender toward it for the sake of God's image
stamped upon it? Can you feel sad at its ruin, its self-
destructiveness, its failure to live up to God's original design?

Travel Wisdom

Sometimes we Christians are condemning of our culture because we exist in a state of culture shock.
Things around us are not what they should be.
Cross-cultural training enables American workers to
cope with the shock waves of disparate foreign customs by teaching that the sure cure for inevitable
frustration, exhaustion, and dismay is to deliberately

start finding what's good in the place you've landed. Focusing on the good, the delightful, or the amazing often releases us from neurotic negative compulsions, and we are suddenly free to enjoy our displacement in another land.

In China, for instance, it is easy to concentrate on impoliteness in public lines (what lines?), or on the people-shoving on public transportation. You might conclude that the Chinese are, by nature, rude and unfriendly. Then you are invited to be a guest in a Chinese home and discover how reserves of warmth and friendliness are lavished upon visitors, friends, and family. Maybe you will be shocked again, but this time by the level of care, attention, hospitality, and gentility you receive in a Chinese home. "*Chi, chi, chi,*" a hostess will say. Eat. Eat. Eat. When you leave, your host will walk you to the door, down the stairs, into the courtyard, down the street, and to the bus stop. "*Ma man zou,*" he will say. Walk slowly. Don't hurry through life. "*Ma man zou.*"

It's easy for clockwork-wound North Americans, when faced with another ethnicity's timetable, to conclude that a certain nationality is slow, lazy, disorganized, or good-for-nothing. In Mexico, high value is put on relationships; it may be more important to be have time for family, to stop and chat on the street with an acquaintance, than to be punctual.

Recently, our youngest son and I grabbed 10 days away in Mexico. A cross-cultural expert, Jeremy's goal was to give me "a real Mexican" exposure—as opposed to a tourist-like skimming of the surface. Having stayed south of the border for several weeks before I arrived, he met me in Guadalajara, the second largest city in Mexico and the source of many of those aspects we North Americans think of as particularly Mexican: mariachi bands, wide sombreros, hat dances, tequila. We stayed in the oldest hotel, built some 300 years ago, in the downtown historic section. We were surrounded on all sides by public squares— *Plaza de la Liberacion*, *Plaza Tapatia*, *Plaza de Armas*, and *Plaza de los Laureles*—all filled with families and strollers, hurrying business people and government officials, food vendors and shoe shiners. In *Plaza de Armas*, the central pavilion is a band shell attractively supported on its rounded sides by bronze art nouveau ladies. Here free concerts are given on Thursday and Sunday evenings, and old women with grandchildren, young lovers, fathers and mothers all gather to listen while busses stop and start, exhausts and horns blow, rush-hour traffic bumps in the streets.

On my bed in Hotel Frances, I would lie awake listening to four different clocks chiming the hour and the quarter-hours. They varied by about two minutes. It was really quite lovely listening to the clocks and bells marking the hour over a short span of time, rather than all at once. When I mentioned this to my son the next morning, he laughed and said, "Oh yes! It's four o'clock, more or less, just about four, maybe, basically four, thereabouts, close enough; right now it's four o'clock, pretty much."

Now, we could have fixated on this time differential as a symptom of something missing in that culture. Instead, we focused on the grace of the Mexican people, their love of family, their festive natures, their marvelous use of explosive color, their music in the streets and on the corners and in the restaurants, courtyards, and municipal squares. Hey, we wanted to enjoy our vacation!

One evening we happened upon a festival in *Plaza Liberacion*. Balloon makers twisted wild-shaped creatures for children. Blasts from air vents caught up balloons and kites and lifted them high above our heads. Vendors sold ice cream and soap bubble kits; a living machine of hundreds of little children cranked out thousands of floating, transparent orbs into the cooling summer night. Papas hoisted little ones to their shoulders, and beautiful, dark-eyed boys and girls chased around the fountain, momentarily losing their parents in the crowd. A musician sang gentle songs under a canvas pavilion as the sun set serenely behind the towers and gilded dome of the *Catedral* . . .

Do we wonder if God loves the earth? At moments like these, you would have to be a fool not to feel the embrace of divine charity for the world and all the people in it.

. . . And the chimes in the clock towers and the bells in the belfries struck the hour, the quarter-hour—more or less, just about, maybe, basically, thereabouts, close enough, pretty much.

Compliment the culture. Find what is beautiful in it. See this with loving eyes. Like my friend, the taxi driver, tell somebody.

Reality Checkpoints

Due to some schedule changes in Mexico, it was necessary to rearrange our departure plans to go home. Since my son speaks fluent Spanish, he went off to the airport, returning several hours later without the business finished. He told me, "I don't think the travel agent at Mexican Airlines was very favorable to our changing these flights; I couldn't even get a smile out of her. There was an awful American ahead of me who was dressing down another agent: 'You say you're in the service industry; you don't know anything about what you're doing. We bring millions of dollars of business down here. . . .'" After this jerk was gone, Jeremy said he felt so bad, he apologized to the young woman for his fellow countryman.

The next morning found us at the same Mexicana customer service counter with the same reserved woman who had been slow to help Jeremy the day before. I put on my best border-crossing demeanor: "I know this is a lot of trouble, but if you could help us make these flight changes, we would be deeply appreciative." She called United Airlines (part of the Star Alliance), which had awarded me the free ticket for accumulated flight mileage; they informed her the supervisor at our end would have to approve the transaction. The time was 11:00 in the morning, and the supervisor was going to lunch. The agent could go ahead and approve this, but we might have problems the day we flew out. The supervisor would be back from lunch at 12:30. I told her that I thought we should do the correct thing, that we didn't mind waiting, and that she was being very helpful to us. Jeremy bought a *USA Today* newspaper and we waited.

Upon returning to the customer service counter, the young woman who had been dealing with the difficult American came on duty. Jeremy smiled and said to her, "I told my mother about the incident yesterday," and he motioned toward me.

"Yes," I said. "When we run across ugly Americans like that, we just say we're from Canada."

At that moment the older woman who was dealing with our ticket changes cracked a smile and the younger woman said, "Yo haf a wun-d'ful son." In short order, we were placed on the flights we needed to get home together—supervisor approved—and our Mexicana agent worked quickly and diligently to arrange for our exchange fees to be reduced. Why? Because Jeremy and I sincerely loved their land, because we had found that basic humanity, that eagerness to please, was something we had in common with the Mexican women helping us.

When you check in at an airline counter, you may be asked for a photo ID. What characteristics make up your personal ID? Are you identified by ready affirmation and an open ear?

Can you, like the apostle Paul, find God even among the idols of a lost culture? Then, can you express to those of this world the connections between their interests and the spiritual realm? Little by little, begin to work on these challenges. Perhaps you too will become a great communicator for the gospel.

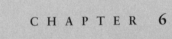

CHAPTER 6

Daniel: The Exile
Who Traveled Light

THEME

Stay Alert to Self-Diminishing Compromises

TEXT

Daniel 1:1–20

APPLICATION 6

Axe the Excess

HAVE YOU ever wondered what kind of women raised the four young Israelite nobles who withstood the luxuries of King Nebuchadnezzar's lavish table? If you are not a woman, or if you are not a mother, you probably never have thought about this. Being both, and having cared for three sons, as well as a son-in-law and four grandsons, I am prone to ponder what kind of mothers gave their children the fortitude to keep their Hebrew identity while in exile in the prosperous court of the Persian conqueror.

What was Daniel's mother like? Was she alive during the account in the opening pages of the book of Daniel? Had she been slaughtered in the conquest, or did she languish in captivity and die of a broken heart? Had she mourned over the beheading of a husband? Exactly what kind of woman instills strength into a young man who grows up to wisely defy the edict of kings, deftly counsel potentates, safely maintain personal integrity in the face of intrigue, danger, and power politics?

We know she was noble. Scripture tells us that Nebuchadnezzar "ordered Ashpenaz, chief of his court officials, to bring in some of the Israelites from the royal family and the nobility" (Daniel 1:3). We might surmise that she was beautiful; attractive parents often bear attractive children, and the Scriptures say Daniel was one of the "young men without any physical defect, handsome" (verse 4).

Using the same kind of reasoning, let us conclude that she was also intelligent, since her son was chosen for "showing aptitude for every kind of learning, well-informed, quick to understand" (verse 4). Probably Daniel's mother was a woman of culture, since one of the qualifications for this conscription was that her son be "qualified to serve in the king's palace."

What we can certainly ascertain is that Daniel's mother kept a kosher kitchen (or oversaw servants who honored the Old Testament dietary restrictions). How else would her son be certain that an alternative diet would keep him fit and healthy enough to compete against the physical condition of any of the other young men in the king's service?

Daniel had influences in his early years that shaped him to be unbreakable, filled with internal resolve. These formed him into one of those remarkable men who stand tall, do not bend when they should not bend, whose identity, even in exiled surroundings, is responsive to molding under the hand of God. I think Daniel had a mother who was a good woman. Many children of nobility are wealthy, spoiled wastrels; this Hebrew youth and his buddies were princes in every sense. At least we know his mother had reared him well. The Scriptures tell us, "Daniel resolved not to defile himself" (verse 8). Here was a young man who had been trained to stay alert to self-diminishing compromises.

What are self-diminishing compromises? They are the little allowances we make for attractive options in our culture, which are not bad in themselves but which, in excess, can threaten our spiritual health. For instance, though there is nothing wrong with food in general, many of us struggle with the reality that too much food, or an overabundance of junk food, can damage our physical condition. What's more, we know that the extra pounds detract from our appearance; we can't seem to control the eating, and our self-image is diminished. The feeding cycle becomes not only a physical and emotional fiasco but a spiritual failure as well. That is why Daniel felt that the rich food of the King's table would defile him.

Application Step: Axe the Excess

Travel theory insists that there are two breeds of packers: people who stuff everything in a suitcase to be prepared for any eventuality and people who travel as light as possible, figuring they will pick up what they need on the road. I am a packer who aspires to the travel-light category but always succumbs to the "what if" over-preparedness of the first group. What if the weather turns cold? What if I have to attend a dressy function at an embassy? What if I can't find the toiletries I need when I run out? What if someone in my traveling party gets sick? Through the years of travel and dragging stuff along behind me, I have developed a case of diagnosed "luggage elbow." Periodically this heals, only to become inflamed when I haul a suitcase, even one on wheels, behind me through too many airports.

My European solo journey was complicated by the fact that although I needed clothes at the beginning of the trip in order to speak before 700 women for five days, the contents of a small rolling suitcase and a carryon bag would have suited me fine for the next three weeks. I hauled two large suitcases, a carryon bag, a satchel with speaking notes, and my large purse throughout the rest of the journey. No wonder I had anxieties over my possessions! I had a lot to keep organized, to yank onto trains before the electric doors shut, to shove under seats and hoist into overhead bins, to tuck around me in sleeper cars shared with three other female passengers—and their belongings. Then I had to scoot all this travel paraphernalia down the narrow aisles of trains along with other passengers moving their luggage, and once I arrived, I had to open my little cart, stack the baggage, secure it so it wouldn't heave from side to side, and make my way to another train track, taxi stand, or elevator. You can imagine what a relief it was to see the faces of people who had come to meet me; they could help me with the purely physical challenges of moving luggage!

When changing trains in Basel, Switzerland, my bags shifted. I tripped on the platform, fell to my knees like an uncoordinated idiot, and had to hastily reload the whole mountain of stuff in order to catch the next train, which was scheduled to depart in all too few minutes. Traveling light truly would have helped me!

Anything wrong with taking suitcases along as you travel? Absolutely not. However, a traveler loses mobility with too much baggage. The application step for this week suggests that you axe the excess. In what area are you not traveling light? We are going to propose three categories for you to examine.

1. Are you focusing too much on possessions?
2. Are you focusing too much on entertainment?
3. Are you focusing too much on activity?

Any excess in these three categories—possessions, entertainment, or activity—can diminish your spiritual health. Nothing is wrong with having material goods, being entertained, or enjoying an active life; again, we are considering the *quantity* of these three things.

A good measurement for determining whether any of these areas is out of control is the how-much question. How much time do I give to shopping for or taking care of the material possessions in my life? How much money do I spend on leisure or pleasure? How much mental engagement is the activity in my life demanding of me? Then we must ask, am I addicted to, obsessed by, compulsive about any of these three? If so, what am I going to do about it?

When our children were young, David and I attempted to control television viewing while teaching our brood of four to be discriminating and analytical viewers. I put a chart on the television, and the kids were to record how much time they spent in front of the set. To nobody's surprise, I myself was the worst offender. How could I possibly teach the children to control *their* viewing if I couldn't control *my* viewing? So, when one of the children dropped the portable set (bought under the deluded theory that we could put it in the closet when we were not using it), we decided not to buy another one. Decades later, I see that this decision was one of the best we ever made for our family. We are one of the few parents I know who raised children without television. The benefits are huge, and I can think of *no* negatives.

However, for five years after the children were grown, our communications ministry produced a daily national television show aired out of Chicago. The production team would tape five half-hour shows one day and five more half-hour shows the next day. How could we possibly evaluate what we were doing if we didn't have a television at home? So we purchased a 36-inch screen. It wasn't long before I discovered that my propensities for addiction were as strong as they had been 20 years before, when we had abandoned the TV.

In time, we moved the television set from the upstairs study, which I pass ten or twenty times a day, to the family room in the basement, to which I go two or three times daily. We chose not to connect it to the antenna, concluding that, for my spiritual health, we could do without. We have a VCR and can watch videos.

My son built a black wooden lock box for his protection when he was in college (before the invention of the V-chip). Due to the self-diminishing compromises that exist for me with excessive television viewing, the black box has now been reestablished. To watch a video, I must get the key, go down to the basement, unlock the box, stoop way over and haul up the electrical panel, plug in the VCR cord—then reverse the process to lock the box again. What once used to be a convenience (just to see what is on) has become an act that requires intentionality on my part. I find I don't want to watch anything *that* much.

The bad habit of too much TV began when I was trying to stave off a too-early bedtime. Now I just go to sleep between 9:00 and 9:30 and get up at 4:00 in the morning! My body functions fine with this pattern, even though people look at me in amazement when they discover the hours I keep.

And, oh, it is wonderful to have that time. In the summer, I garden for a few hours in the long evening light; the sewing machine is out again and I'm beginning to work with fabric. I'm reading several books a week. My mind is not distracted by visual snippets or the mental flotsam of totally unnecessary television information. The pop song "57 Channels (And Nothin' On)" states it well; it's amazing how much I don't need to know about the trivia of this world.

Mostly, my soul was being diminished by the dooming cycle: "I know I shouldn't watch so much television. I'll just relax for an hour before doing other stuff. Is it 11:00 already? I hate these late-night talk shows; let's just see who the guests are tonight. Oh, is that old movie on? I've never watched it before. Lord, did I spend the whole night in front of the television? Help me not to waste this part of my life! Why can't I just say no?"

You may be familiar with this cycle in a variety of formulas. Maybe for you it's the adrenaline boost that comes from shopping or the painkiller from having so full a calendar you don't have to think about the troubles you don't know how to solve. What area in your life, perfectly innocent, has the potential to diminish your soul when it becomes excessive? What area is the Holy Spirit nudging you to change? What keeps you from developing a rich relationship with God? This is where you are carrying too much baggage that diminishes the mobility of your journey as an alien and stranger in the world. You need to lighten the load. You need to axe the excess.

Travel Wisdom

Our youngest son, Jeremy, was born with cross-cultural genes. His need for dips into cultures foreign to our own manifested themselves early when, at fifteen years of age, he cajoled us into letting him spend a summer in Japan. Since then, his trips around the world have been extensive. He is now a department supervisor in a small, not-for-profit office that assists internationals with the complications and legalities of resettlement in the United States. At this point in his life, Jeremy is a paralegal, an immigration specialist with a grasp on immigration law so extensive it fills a technical manual almost six inches thick.

Travel of any kind is educational, but it is the long stays in other countries that really inform North Americans about the valuable gifts other cultures can give. While teaching English to university students in China, Jeremy and his team lived for two years in the Guest House of the Petroleum Institute in the city of Nanchong, in the middle of Sechuan Province. Though the city numbered more than 500,000, these English teachers were the rare western faces that Chinese population would see. Two years is long enough to begin to understand the richness of cultures that are not overdeveloped (although China is furiously working at it).

Latin Americans call North Americans *exclavos al reloj*, slaves to time. The slower pace of life in many places of the world gives those who live in them a sense of proportion; there is an overwhelming richness in not having to fill every moment with activity. Jeremy learned that when his Chinese students asked, "Would you like to do something?" they meant right then and for the next six hours. The typical North American response would be, "Sure, that's great. I'll give you a call. Let me get something down on my calendar." And the unstated intent too often is *If I get around to it*. The students' invitation meant, *Why don't we spend time together—now?*

Visiting with a Bosnian family he was helping to resettle through a local church outreach, Jeremy came to understand that an invitation to a meal meant eating, then visiting for the entire afternoon or evening. You do not rush relationships; you give them time, you laugh, you converse, you think aloud together, you tell stories. The art of personal inter-action—which we are losing in our fast-paced, stressed-out, overscheduled modern life—is still cul-tivated in these places.

Is your soul being diminished because of the lack of enriching friendships? "Walk slowly" *(ma man zou)*, as the Chinese say. What can you give up so you will have time to reinsert the things you have lost?

We enjoyed dinner this past fall with Dr. Marva Dawn when she was the visiting scholar for the grad-uate school at Wheaton College. Her book, *Keeping the Sabbath Wholly*, is a theological treatment of the Sabbath principle for moderns. For us, it was won-derful to connect with someone who has carefully developed a Sabbath practice. In our conversation, Dr. Dawn spoke of two churches in a town in Minnesota that decided to take the concept of a sab-batical year seriously. Both congregations drastically reduced their calendars, keeping only the Sunday morning worship services and any meetings that would be conducive to developing relationships. At the end of the experiment, they discovered that most activities on the church calendars were unnecessary. When the schedules were reduced in this fashion, the life of the community actually grew in its connectedness, deepened in its commitment, and experienced the life of Christ more richly in its midst.

What excess do you need to axe to allow time for relationships, for growing your soul and your intellect? Axe the excess. Stay alert to self-diminishing compromises.

It is true, most of us carry too much baggage. This awkward stuff keeps us aliens and strangers in the world from moving freely. Our possessions possess us. Our finances determine our present and future. Our souls are midgets with no room to grow.

Jeremy tells about taking a bus trip over a weekend with a Chinese friend. Carefully packing only what would fit in a backpack, he was surprised when the friend exclaimed, "Are you taking all that?" The other young man had packed a change of underwear and a toothbrush. Now *that's* traveling light!

Last summer David and I and our daughter and son-in-law shared dinner with some acquaintances from the entertainment community in Hollywood. We had rented a cottage in a summer community on Lake Michigan, and this was one of those rare, long, unhurried dinners (the kind after which people invariably ask, "Why don't we do this more often?"). One couple worked as executives at Disney; the wife was at that time the personal assistant to

Michael Eisner, the CEO of the multi-conglomerate enterprise. The responsibility of this woman was to coordinate all the Disney products as they were introduced in marketplaces around the world, which obviously required international travel.

My ears perked up. Here was someone of proven administrative capabilities. I kept seeing myself pushing two suitcases, my satchel, purse, and carryon down the narrow corridors of those European trains. Certainly, this woman had reduced packing to a science. Sure enough, no matter where the trip, this high-level Disney employee never took more than what she could put in a wheeled suitcase small enough to fit in the overhead bin of an airplane. Color-coordinated clothes and one change of shoes, in addition to what she was wearing, were the rule. Then the whole dinner table was introduced to a delightful lecture on the packing strategy of rolling garments: Nothing is packed flat. This, she insisted, reduces wrinkles and provides more room in a small case. So we spent the evening making jokes and smart comments about rolling jackets, raincoats, skirts, blouses, and so on. (The humor level was set on high, as comedy writers were also present.)

Despite our nonchalance about this *pro bono* expertise, my next trip found me attempting to apply this newly acquired travel science. I limited myself to one roll-on suitcase that would fit in the overhead bin—and a roomy carryon, I admit, but no purse. I attempted to color-coordinate my outfits and controlled the compulsion to pack a variety of shoes. And I rolled my clothes. Sure enough, the garments were less wrinkled when I unpacked them, and it seemed as though I had more space in the bag.

I also gained simplicity: no waiting at the baggage counter, no worrying if my luggage would arrive, no complicated decisions about which clothes to choose. And I found the welcome feeling of competence from having reduced my normally excessive baggage habit. What a relief not to hear myself say, "Oh, dear. I've over-packed again!"

Great saints always strip their living to a level of simplicity. They are attempting to achieve a higher good, and whatever inhibits this must be excised. Championship runners consider how their clothes, even how their hairstyles, will create wind resistance and delay their race by the milliseconds that can set a gold-medal winner apart from the rest of the pack. The Psalmist declared, "I run in the path of your commands, for you have set my heart free" (Psalm 119:32). These are examples we all should follow.

Reality Checkpoint

The fine print on the back of every traditional airplane ticket spells out passenger terms that protect airlines from liability in case anything goes wrong. One section explains the regulations concerning baggage—how much a traveler is allowed to take on the flight, how large carryon luggage may be and how many pieces, and what is considered excess. What happens when you're bringing along too much? "An excess fee or handling charge will be collected for each piece of baggage over the designated free baggage allowance and for each piece of oversize or overweight baggage. In addition, a handling charge will be collected for special items such as bicycles, surfboards, household pets, etc."

Take a moment to consider: What price are you paying for the excess baggage you are dragging along on your journey? Is it an amount you can afford, a wise use of your resources?

Perhaps Daniel's mother was the one who taught him the principles of traveling light. We can learn from his example, but there is another exile from whom we can learn even more.

The most economic traveler who ever crossed the face of the earth was Jesus Christ. Here was an alien and stranger who knew how to travel light. He had no home to call his own, no place he could count on to lay his head. He owned one seamless garment, a cloak for which Roman soldiers threw dice to win. Do you want to learn how to make your way as a displaced one on the earth? Look to Jesus. He owned nothing, yet the entire world was his. The saying is true: Wealth consists not in having great possessions but in having few wants. What is burdening the flight of your soul? Cast off the cargo and see how high you can soar.

CHAPTER 7

Ruth: The Refugee
Who Risked Everything

THEME

Risk Everything for God and His People

TEXT

Ruth 1:1–18

APPLICATION 7

Run the Risk

BEFORE THE Berlin Wall was torn down in 1989, the news services carried frequent stories like that of the three refugees who swam a river to escape from East Germany to West Germany. They chose a season when tourists crowded the resort area on the border from which they made a desperate bid for freedom. "Don't shoot! Don't shoot!" screamed the young woman to border guards waving automatic rifles, "A baby is in my body! A baby is in my body!"

Have you ever wondered what motivates such dangerous journeys? Have you ever asked yourself how bad it would have to get before you risked your life for a chance at some intangible ideal?

Throughout the long history of mankind, intolerance, persecution, and war have generated mass movements of frightened, weary people. The very word *refugee* is translated from the French *refugie* and dates back 300 years to the Protestant Huguenots who fled religious repression. The U.S. Committee for Refugees reports that more than 35 million people are refugees or internally displaced persons— men, women, and children who have had to flee to save their lives. No one knows whether the world now has proportionately more refugees than in former times, or whether we are just more aware of desperate, suffering people because of media attention around the world. We *do* know that refugees have always been.

Relief sources say the world has produced over 100 million refugees since World War II. With those stable historical figures as a foundation, let us build a framework to look more closely at the miserable, forced evacuations that followed those years.

In the five months after Germany's surrender, the United Nations repatriated 7 million displaced persons, not counting the 12 million mostly European refugees who fled their homes during the war itself. Entire refugee populations were exchanged or ejected. Among them were thousands of Russians, who in some cases were forcibly sent back to the Soviet Union. Many ended up in Stalin's slave camps.

Other East Europeans refused to live under Soviet control or domination. One million people from Russia, Czechoslovakia, Hungary, and other eastern countries poured into refugee camps in 1946. The partition of India in 1947 produced millions of Muslim and Hindu refugees, fleeing religious strife. In the Middle East, the creation of Israel in 1948 absorbed most of Europe's remaining Jewish population—those who had survived the Holocaust. But the conflict between Israelis and Arabs produced a new crop of homeless, about 750,000 Palestinians. Since the end of the war in 1945 up to the building of the Berlin Wall in 1961, more than 3.75 million East Germans fled to the West.

Statistics are one thing, but in purely human terms it is impossible to describe the quantity of suffering experienced when such huge population displacement occurs. In April 1945, upon reaching the death camp of Belen, a London war correspondent of *The Times* wrote, "It is my duty to describe something beyond the imagination of mankind." The same response can aptly be applied to all the inhumane situations since that have propelled families with small children, men and women, and the elderly to flee for their lives in order to find some kind of promise of safety, of sanctuary.

In 1951, the United Nations High Commissioner for Refugees was established to deal with the 1.25 million refugees still in Europe. But the early 1970s marked the beginning of the worst refugee crises in modern times. Population displacement—caused by turmoil in Southeast Asia, Afghanistan, Africa, and Latin America—continued. At the time I am writing, Africa is the world's most volatile continent, with war between Ethiopia and Eritrea; regional fighting in Congo-Kinshasa; civil unrest in Sudan, Burundi, and Angola; armed insurgencies ruthlessly tearing apart Sierra Leone and Uganda; violent political chaos in Somalia; and possible renewed hostilities in Liberia and Congo-Brazzaville.

It is estimated that in Colombia, South America, one in 40 people have been forced to leave home. In the Balkans, an estimated 1.7 million remain displaced—nearly one-tenth of the combined population of Bosnia, Herzegovina, Croatia, and the Federal

Republic of Yugoslavia. In the aftermath of devastation in East Timor, more than 75 percent of the population has been displaced, and more than 70 percent of all private housing, public buildings, and utilities have been destroyed by pro-Indonesian militia.

In light of this ever-present anguish, it is intriguing to note that the Bible chronicles the plight of refugees. In a sense, Adam and Eve became refugees after their expulsion from the Garden of Eden. The children of Israel, in their flight from Egypt and during 40 years of wanderings through the desert, were certainly refugees. If an *internally displaced person* is defined as "someone who has been forced from his/her home for refugee-like reasons but remains within the borders of his/her own country," then David, hiding from King Saul in the hills and caves of the wilderness, could be classified as one. Eventually, the dispersion of the entire population of Israel took place under a cruel, conquering army, and this history is a study in the tragic consequences of forced migrations.

Lift the laments of the Old Testament prophets over the siege, defeat, and dispersion of the people of Jerusalem and, except for the modern weaponry capable of mass destruction, you can press it like a template over the misery and suffering in contemporary times. Thousands of frightened people fleeing to sanctuary appear disturbingly familiar—very Old Testament, if I might say.

A Character Heroine

A category of refugees the technical definition does not cover is of those who become displaced persons because of love. One book in the Bible focuses on this particular status. It's the story of an individual who became a refugee because of her personal choice, not because of any "well-founded fear of persecution." This refugee tells the one she loves, "Don't urge me to leave you or to turn back from you. Where you go I will go, and where you stay I will stay. Your people will be my people and your God my God" (Ruth 1:16). This exquisite pledge of love, of course, is the vow of Ruth to her mother-in-law, Naomi.

The book of Ruth is a story of great risks taken for the sake of love. It's the story of love between Ruth the refugee and Boaz, the great man of the community. Their first meeting at the gleaning of the fields is recorded; he has instructed his foreman to take care for her and tells Ruth to stay safely with his servant girls. "Why have I found such favor in your eyes that you notice me—a foreigner?" she asks the rich landowner, astonished at his kindness (Ruth 2:10).

Bethlehem's gossip has told Boaz about Ruth's fidelity, how she followed her mother-in-law, left her own father and mother and homeland to live with people she did not know. In a sense, Boaz says to the young woman that he admires how she has risked all she has for the sake of her love for Naomi. Then he pronounces this fantastic blessing: "May you be richly rewarded by the Lord, the God of Israel, under whose wings you have come to take refuge" (verse 12).

Yes, the book of Ruth is the story of risking everything for love; it is also the study of a relationship between a young woman and an older woman and the restoration of the older one not only to her homeland or to the village of her childhood, but to the blessing and embrace of her God. Upon returning from Moab, to which she had fled to escape famine, and after leaving the bodies of her husband and two grown sons buried in that foreign soil, Naomi tells her neighbors, "Don't call me Naomi," which means *pleasant*. "Call me Mara," which means *bitter*, "because the Almighty has made my life very bitter. I went away full, but the Lord has brought me back empty" (Ruth 1:20–21).

As we know, the story of Ruth, the refugee who risked everything, has a happy ending. "So Boaz took Ruth and she became his wife . . . and she gave birth to a son" (Ruth 4:13).

Then the women of Bethlehem said to Naomi,

"Praise be to the Lord, who this day has not left you without a kinsman-redeemer. May he become famous throughout Israel! He will renew your life and sustain you in your old age. For your daughter-in-law, who loves you and who is better to you than seven sons, has given him birth." (Ruth 4:14–15)

It is the women of the community who name the newborn. They call him *Obed*. As a grandmother who experiences ecstatic joy over her grandchildren, I can imagine the hope and health this brought to Naomi's shriveled heart. "Naomi has a son," the women call to one another, passing along the good news. "Naomi has a son."

Having risked everything for the sake of love, Ruth sees the fulfillment of the blessing of Boaz. God gives her a husband of stature, a mother-in-law whose grief is mending, respect in the rejoicing community, a healthy baby boy . . . and, amazingly, a place in the lineage of King David and the ancestry of Jesus Christ.

Because of Ruth's choice, her difficult decision to become a refugee for the sake of love, she lived to see the fruit of her sacrifice. Years down the road, she would be able to say to herself, *It was worth it all*. But little did she know when she abandoned family and country, little did she know when she chose to become a refugee because of her loyal compassion, that God would include her in his master plan beyond the capability of her imaginings.

Ruth has something to say to us Christians of the twenty-first century. We need to learn to become refugees because of love; we need to learn to risk everything for God and his people. Oh, we say we want to serve God. We say we want to live lives that are spiritually significant, that count for something. But we're not willing, most of us, to turn our backs on these familiar things that tie us—these homes, these places, these possessions, these attitudes, these petty habits. We're not willing to turn our backs on the old gods. We refuse to journey into unknown lands, the spiritual territories of prayer and testing that document our status as aliens on the earth.

Comfort is the god most western Christians worship. Our goal is to live comfortably, to give our children the comforts of life, to retire comfortably, to die comfortably . . . all despite the fact that Jesus says nothing about comfort either being the goal or the measurement of true discipleship.

How often have you heard someone say, in so many words, "I don't want much. I just want to be comfortable"? The problem with this concept is that when it is dictated by the environment in which we live rather than by a Christian ethic, the standard of comfort continues to rise with the result that we want more and more. And then we are not willing to risk comfort, to give joyfully and sacrificially, to open our homes to strangers in need, to take off as short-term missionaries, to choose a lower-paying job because it affords us the opportunity to serve the world, to expose ourselves to theological systems that might shatter our smug suppositions.

Because there is no risk attached to our Christian experience, we are ordinary, everyday, ineffectual Christians with feet firmly planted in heathen, Moabite territory. We are formed by the pagan society around us. We see no healing coming from our lives into the lives of others. We bring no blessing to the communities in which we live. We achieve no great loves. We are like Orpah, the daughter-in-law who kissed Naomi and went back to her people. We are the sisters-in-law who return to the comfortable, familiar terrain—to the wooden idols made by human hands—and are never heard of again. Yes, we are never heard of again.

Application Step: Run the Risk

In order to thrive spiritually in this life's journey across the earth, we are going to have to learn to run the risk in some areas of our living. The principle is true no matter how it is stated: No pain, no gain. Nothing ventured, nothing gained. No risk, no reward. Yet we Christians of the western world know so little in terms of sacrifice that the concept of risking anything for the sake of God is almost foreign to our thinking.

In the early church, to die for one's faith was an ideal. In time, as the church became more institutionalized, red martyrdom, which ended with the spilling of one's lifeblood, gave way to green martyrdom, in which devoted followers removed themselves from the world into the desert or monastic communities in order to more fully explore the depths of the human experience, to become scientists of the soul. Today, though countless Christians across the world are having to decide if they will sacrifice security, their health, or the future for their family if they make an open commitment to Christian discipleship, we North American believers are needing to conduct serious risk assessments in order to live counter to our culture.

In his remarkable book *Redeeming the Routines: Bringing Theology to Life,* Robert Banks challenges modern Christians to apply our belief in Christ to the routines of common duties and responsibilities. How do our convictions influence what we eat, how we dress, the way we sleep, where we live, what work we choose, or how we bathe, commute, converse, exercise, and form daily habits? This is an ambitious study that needs to be discussed in depth by groups of committed Christians, but the essence of the author's premise is that applied theology turns your life upside down.[1]

First of all, what areas, if any, are you willing to risk for God? Can you risk your home or your car? Are you willing to put your reputation at risk? What about your income? Have you ever felt you were being asked to put your health or safety at risk for the sake of the gospel? Are you willing to risk the security of your family, or of members of your family? What about the comfortable future you have been planning for yourself? If it were required of you for the sake of Christ, would you risk your life? In a culture that worships comfort, the radical results of answering these questions from a Christian viewpoint subvert the social norms.

Throughout the history of the church, Christians who understood their status as aliens and strangers in the world put every single one of the above categories at risk in order to follow Christ, advance his kingdom, and make a stand for justice and morality in an evil, fallen world.

When I conduct a personal assessment of willingness to risk, I find that David and I risked our safety and that of our children when we moved into the strife-torn inner city of Chicago in the 1970s to plant a church when other congregations were closing their doors and fleeing. We risked the good opinion of status-quo, conservative Christianity when we broke the usual worship forms in order to relate to the tumultuous culture of those times. We sent our children to non-Christian colleges, into secular environments that tested their faith and forced their own risk-taking over choices of mates and professions. We've risked financial security by not having a savings plan and by giving any excess to those in need. We've remortgaged our home and turned over inheritance disbursements to keep our present ministry afloat until it could stabilize its identity and determine God's calling for its future. We have risked in many areas.

However, I find as we age that I am tempted to seek comfort. Risk-taking is never easy, though after a lifetime one might expect it to become habitual. I find that for me it does not. The personal risk assessment I am undergoing at this moment is raising questions about where I will place my security as I age. Am I going to trust in God to shelter us, to provide for us when feebleness begins to set into our minds and bodies? Am I going to trust in the one who has never abandoned us, who has never turned his back on us? Or am I going to spend a great deal of time right now securing financial stability for a future that I cannot really foresee?

Today's culture, modern financial planners, and our own family members will say we are foolish to be so ill-prepared for the vagaries of our last decades. And yet this has been a long journey, this life-migration into becoming totally dependant upon God. It has been a long pilgrimage into trust and the exercise of faith. Shall we abandon the lessons God has taught us because of a new stage of life?

I am struggling to answer this question: *God, is there an area of my life in which you might be calling me to run the risk?* What kind of wrestling matches will this same question impose on your soul?

Moab is the ancient name for the modern country of Jordan. Years ago, I encountered a remarkable man I think about from time to time when spiritual risk-management questions occur. A bright and promising Jordanian, he had been given a scholarship and sponsorship through the missionary community in Amman to attend a denominational college in the States, where he could receive a degree in social work. When I met him decades later, he had graduated from college, earned higher degrees in his field, and was the founder and catalyst for a social outreach program for Palestinian refugees evacuated from their homes on the West Bank and attempting to make some kind of life for themselves in exile.

Host countries that receive waves of fleeing populations can hardly manage the pure physical needs of these refugee groups, let alone provide any kind of future for them. Returning from the States, this man founded a social services department of which he became head in the Jordanian University. Then he established an extensive program for Palestinian refugees, helping them to resettle, find jobs, or receive training. The group with which I was touring visited his school for refugee children, where he shared his dream and what had been accomplished so far: clinics, women's health groups, and assistance systems. Since I'd dragged through countless refugee camps, many of them Palestinian camps in Israel, I was impressed. The genius of the program was that social services majors at the university, under this man and other professors' direction, helped to run the outreaches as a practicum for their field of study.

"Is he a Christian?" I asked, wondering about the missionary connection and the stateside denominational college.

"Oh, no," replied the woman who was translating for me. "He is Muslim and rather cool to Christianity, I think." I discovered, upon further questioning, that while the president of that school of higher learning had seen the promise in this young

Arab, had taken the international student under his wing, and was gratefully considered by the young man to be a mentor, the years in the States had been lonely. The "good Christian community" had quietly ostracized him, excluded him from social gatherings, allowed him to spend holidays alone in the dormitory, and, most importantly, kept their daughters from dating him. (I could understand why. He was tall, dark, strikingly handsome, and would stand out in any crowd.)

I always wonder what might have happened if someone had run the risk and included this individual in the social calendar, if someone had risked getting past his Muslim faith and attempted to see the brilliant young man. What if good mothers had tried planning parties where he was included, had brought him home (despite their unmarried daughters) for holidays, or taken him to the beach for vacations? What if Christian hospitality had been applied at its riskiest but most scriptural essence: "I want you to share your food with the hungry and to welcome poor wanderers into your homes" (Isaiah 58:7a, NLT)?

What difference could all this risk-taking have made in the life of one young man, a Jordanian Arab, a prime mover with enormous pragmatic compassion for the refugee?

What kind of risk is God asking you to take for him right now? Are you willing to be a refugee who risks everything for love's sake? God risked everything, his beloved Son, for you.

Reality Checkpoints

Three types of insurance are offered by agents for those who travel: trip-cancellation insurance, medical coverage, and lost luggage coverage. In addition, many credit cards offer automatic flight insurance against death or dismemberment in case of a plane crash. A question that might help you analyze how culturally bound you are to this world is: As one of God's aliens on earth, with an ultimate heavenly destination in mind, who is holding your traveler's insurance?

Does the stock market hold your insurance? Or are you invested in the opinions of your friends and neighbors? Does your workplace keep your trust, with the status and financial returns you receive from it? Could it be reliance on your family that helps you feel safe? (They could be taken at any time, you know.)

Or have you, like Ruth, thrown everything into the hands of the God you're just beginning to know? Take the risk. Become a refugee of love. Leave your past, with all its securities and comfort, and place yourself at the feet of the Beloved who leads his people.

CHAPTER 8

Christ: Our True Safe Haven

THEME

Fix Your Eyes on Eternity with Jesus

TEXT

Hebrews 12:1–29

APPLICATION 8

Eye the Prize

$\mathbf{S}$OMETIMES THE havens to which we flee become more treacherous than the places from which we escape. What we think will be a sanctuary becomes threatening. What we think will protect us leaves us more vulnerable. Many refugees, escaping for their lives, discover that the safe havens they have struggled to reach are not so safe.

In 1994, for instance, the U.S. government tried to handle two waves of Cuban and Haitian sea migrations by establishing a temporary holding facility called a "safe haven," for refugees at the Naval base in Guantanamo Bay, Cuba. In the language of the international laws establishing protections for fleeing peoples, there is a concept of "humane deterrence." This halts migrations that threaten to overwhelm border countries and promises to provide shelter, protection, and basic provisions for temporary periods.

However, in many situations worldwide, refugees are placed in settings that are unnecessarily harsh and isolating, with little promise of future help. Haitians were told, "You cannot resettle in the United States. If you want to go back, the Coast Guard will take you there. If you seek temporary protection, you will be provided with the basics—shelter, food, and medical care. But you will not be given money or allowed to work outside the camp."

The problem with "safe havens" is that, while they help receiving countries in situations where mass population displacement is occurring, the strict legalities established do not entirely protect the refugees.

In Guantanamo, Haitian refugees were kept in minimally hospitable conditions with no possibility of resettlement in the States. Then many were returned to Haiti forcibly.

When the case of the Haitian refugees was rapidly contested by the Haitian Refugee Center, the U.S. court ruled, "We have determined that these migrants are without legal rights that are cognizable in the courts of the United States." This ruling was possible because the refugees were being detained in a "safe haven" on non-U.S. soil, although that Naval base is clearly not under Cuban jurisdiction.

Representatives of non-government humanitarian agencies in Guantanamo reported on the undue militarization of the camp personnel. World Relief personnel testified to an overwhelming combat presence, with soldiers equipped with riot gear and armed with clubs and automatic weapons. "Given the fear that armed military personnel evoke in most Haitians," one said, "there is little wonder that those undergoing the first full day of processing experienced the full physical effect of terror."[1]

Many, with tears in their eyes and despite their protests, were forcibly sent back to Haiti. The coercive repatriation of Haitian refugees indicates that the United States in this case—and with what many consider shaky legal precedent—willfully violated international law.

This "safe haven" failure has occurred in various places around the world. Granted the enormous complexities of materially and politically managing the mass exodus of traumatized populations, sanctuary was nevertheless effectively withheld by the European community, who refused to receive civilians fleeing from Bosnia during the war with Kosovo. One observer lamented, "By sealing all escape routes and means of refuge, European governments are trapping refugees and displaced people in besieged cities and regions and placing them in the crossfire between warring forces."[2]

Let me now attempt to make all this information personal. Take a child in your life whom you love. Imagine walking miles with frightened neighbors and playmates, carrying whatever supplies you can. Imagine trying to find a place to sleep, with the thought that hostile troops are behind you. Imagine needing food. Think of your teenage son or grandson deported with your husband and his father to the men's camp. Think of hearing gunshots. Think of dealing with the stories of torture. Think of the hazards of rape and mayhem.

Think of how different people deal with crises. Not many are noble or self-sacrificing; many are not even concerned for others when there is plenty. What will they do when there is scarcity? What if, in the mass migrations, you become separated from your aging parents? How will you get needed medicine for your family? What if you have seen a loved one murdered and had to move along, abandoning that dear and broken body without burial, for the sake of preserving the lives of the rest of your family?

Consider the worst scenario you can imagine involving friends and family. Millions of people, all over the world, are facing situations like it—except that for them it is worse because it is real. It is horrific because it isn't a fleeting, terrible moment in the mind; it goes on day after day, year after year.

And now, imagine another scene. You are fleeing your country. Your family is straggling behind you, in all the bleakness of your collective desperation and hunger and weariness, and you come upon . . . open arms. You meet One who welcomes you, feeds and nurtures you, accepts you in all your raggedness and destitution—and makes you his own. You find a safe haven, the true safe haven, Christ our Lord.

Application Step: Eye the Prize

The refugee is a window through whom we can view our own status and consider the false illusion that we are safe and protected, that our lives will never be at risk due to forces beyond our control.

Have you ever fled to a safe place, only to discover that sanctuary was an illusion? Did you marry a man or a woman you thought would give the kind of stability that was never present in your family of origin, only to discover hidden areas of dysfunction that were, if not life-threatening, personality-destroying?

Did you run to a church with a community life that seemed to encourage self-expression, only to find beneath the surface a toxic legalism that judged you according to a code of extrascriptural morays?

Have you taken a job offering positional prestige and financial security, only to find you were expected to function in a way that threatened to destroy your personal integrity? Have you taken a stand against immorality, trusting to those who promised to back your righteous protest, only to discover you were betrayed and your professional life was in ruins?

Has someone you trusted betrayed you? Do you know what it means to be abandoned and left to survive by your own wits when promised safety nets were discarded? If you haven't, you will. This is the nature of what it means to be human on the earth.

In a remarkable way, the alien and stranger status that the Scriptures warn each Christian to remember is the very boundary that keeps us from total despondency when we find the safe haven we thought would be there for us is closed or dangerous beyond words.

In fact, God often uses these desperate passages to remind us that, while we are in the world, we are not of the world. You think you have finances enough to keep you secure; then a loved one succumbs to a terminal disease that no money in the world can prevent or cure. You build a position of influence in a community where with one phone call you can open

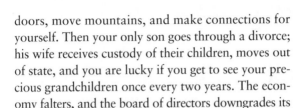

doors, move mountains, and make connections for yourself. Then your only son goes through a divorce; his wife receives custody of their children, moves out of state, and you are lucky if you get to see your precious grandchildren once every two years. The economy falters, and the board of directors downgrades its management team in your corporation. After years of promotions and advancements, you are out of a job.

As hard as these circumstances are, you had forgotten that you do not belong to this world; now you remember that you are an alien and a stranger on the earth. You are journeying to a better place, compared with which every earthly haven is only an illusion. As Hebrews 12:28 reminds us: "Therefore, since we are receiving a kingdom that cannot be shaken, let us be thankful."

Our assignment, the application that will make unbearable life passages bearable, is to "Eye the Prize." The better country where there is enough for all—where peace and justice reign, where no outcasts exist, where no refugees claw for bread or plead for water, where no child dies of malnutrition or abuse, where despots no longer rule, where ruthless brigands can no longer exploit or maim or rape or kill—this shining country is just ahead. We see glimmers of it in perfect but transitory moments here on earth; the treasures of this world, its pleasures, are not of that other, shimmering land. One day you will cross that border-river. Like Christian in *Pilgrim's Progress*, you will come to that Celestial City, to Mount Zion, to the heavenly Jerusalem, the city of the living God. You have come to thousands upon thousands of angels in joyful assembly, to the church of the firstborn, whose names are written in heaven. You have come to God, the judge of all men, to the spirits of righteous men made perfect, to Jesus, the mediator of a new covenant. (Hebrews 12:22–24)

In this exquisite territory, there are no displaced persons, no mass migrations, no refugees.

The Ultimate Character Hero

How do we "Eye the Prize" so we will not forget our alien condition or our stranger designation? Well, as remarkable as heaven is, that far-off beautiful country is not the prize. Surprised? It is only the reward for fixing our eyes on the prize. The prize to be won is Jesus Christ. In truth, he is the only safe haven we Christians will ever have. Hebrews tells us that Jesus is our example:

Let us fix our eyes on Jesus, the author and per-fecter of our faith, who for the joy set before him endured the cross, scorning its shame, and sat down at the right hand of the throne of God. Consider him who endured such opposition from sinful men, so that you will not grow weary and lose heart. (Hebrews 12:2–3)

What was the joy that was set before Christ? Was it the glories of heaven? Experiencing the pleasure of an unfallen Paradise?

No. The joy set before him was our redemption. Christ kept his eyes on the pure rapture of the thought of becoming our Sanctuary, our Hiding Place, and our Salvation. Christ understands the terror and displacement of every refugee. He came unto his own, and they knew him not. He is the original Displaced Person. He was brutalized, tortured, and murdered outside the city walls. He never forgot the reality of the beauty of the one true kingdom, the heavenly place that was his ultimate home. The pleasures of this earthly passage—the treasures men die for, kill for, torture for—were not treasures to him. His death provides the only sanctuary we can count on, the only zone where our souls will be protected. Jesus Christ, the one who transcends all cultures, is the only Safe Haven we humans can count on.

In the musical *Fiddler on the Roof*, the Jews of Anatevka, a little Russian village, are being dispersed. It is a forced evacuation. "Where are you going?" says Tevye to an old acquaintance.

"We're going to Chicago in America. Where are you going?"

"We're going to New York in America. We'll be neighbors!"

The whole outline of preparing for displacement, in the last scenes of the film, includes volumes of wisdom communicated in the song of the community, a song of longing, of reality and lament, a song of every displaced person for all time:

Anatevka, Anatevka, tumble-down, workaday
  Anatevka. . . .
What do we leave? Nothing much.
Only Anatevka, underfed, overworked Anatevka.
Where else would Sabbath be so sweet? . . .
Where I know every face I meet. . . .
I belong to Anatevka, dear little village, little
  town of mine.

For the Christian, any place of familiarity, where we think we know what we know, is only an illusion; one little paper can evict us. We can be forcibly dispersed from security. Really, there is no safe place on earth. Truthfully, though we long for the comfortable, it is not to be compared to the glory that we will one day know. Discomfort is a good companion. It reminds us that we are the displaced people on the earth, aliens on our way to a glorious kingdom.

"Where are you going?"

"To that Bright City. Where are you going?"

"Oh, I'm going there, too. We'll be neighbors!"

If you long to be more than a survivor, drudging out existence in this holding camp of the world, if you yearn to thrive spiritually, you must remember (and never forget) that you do not belong here. Lift your eyes to Christ. Keep his example continually in view. He is the horizon toward which we are journeying. He is the fixed perimeter. He is the brilliant star that leads the way at night.

Reality Checkpoint

Having the right documents is always important for international travel. Many refugees have fled across borders without time enough to get the documentation that proves they are who they say they are. Sometimes this means they are officially classified as stateless, having no homeland they can prove is their own.

Check your More than Survivor card. Keep it at hand. Notice from time to time your temporary address. This is the "Anatevka" of your existence—one that is fragile, temporary, and from which you can be displaced. Always remember your permanent address, the place toward which you are traveling. Write it down so you will never forget during this difficult, tedious, and seemingly unending transit. The Sabbath that begins when eternity dawns, when you finally reach your true home, will be sweeter than you could ever imagine.

The story is told of the missionary who returned home toward the end of her life after having spent years serving the Lord in a foreign country. She kept thinking, as the train on which she was riding approached her town, *Is there anyone here who even remembers who I am?* The anxiety caused by this question began to mount as she counted on one hand the people still alive from the community church that had helped to support her during the many years of her service. The financial support had been steady, but letters and visits from people who knew her as a young woman had dwindled through the years.

As the train approached her town, she had another uncomfortable thought. Though she had wired ahead, would there be anyone to meet her at the station?

However, as the engine slowed, she could see a large crowd gathered on the platform. A band was playing a rousing march. "Welcome Home" signs bobbed over everyone's heads, and children chased each other around, waving banners.

The missionary's heart began to pound. Was this all for her? She couldn't believe it! Quickly, she gathered her few things and, as she was making her way down the aisle, she heard a huge shout go up from the gathered throng.

A distinguished middle-aged man stepped down from her car, waving his arms and smiling broadly. The missionary later learned that he was a local boy who had made good, had become a successful national politician, and was visiting his family as he journeyed to another part of the country.

Disappointed, the elderly woman sat down again on the edge of her seat, trying to catch her breath. She could hear the band playing and the people cheering. *How foolish,* she thought, *to believe that anyone, any group of people that size, would come to welcome me home.*

At that moment, she heard the inner voice, the one she had come to know so well through her decades of service—through dangers and toils, through loneliness and hard-won, rarely celebrated successes. *My dear,* it said. *You haven't come home yet. You haven't come home.*

Endnotes

Introduction
1. Dallas Willard, *The Spirit of the Disciplines: Understanding How God Changes Lives* (New York: Harper & Row, Publishers, Inc., 1988) *ix*.

Chapter 1
1. "The 'Lectric Law Library's Lexicon on Refugee." 'Lectric Law Library Reference Room. February, 1999 <http://222.lectlaw.com/def2/q023.htm>.
2. "Ben's Guide to U.S. Government." Superintendent of Documents, U.S. Government Printing Office. December 6, 1999 <http://bensguide.gpo.gov/9-12/citizenship/oath.html>.

Chapter 2
1. Flannery O'Connor, "The Displaced Person," *The Complete Stories* (New York: Farrar, Straus and Giroux, 1971) 195–235.
2. François Fenelon, *Christian Perfection* (Minneapolis, Minn.: Dimension Books, 1975) 192.
3. Ronald Sanders, *Shores of Refuge: A Hundred Years of Jewish Emigration* (New York: Schocken Books, 1988) 568.

Chapter 3

1. Joe Kidd, "Bag Ladies plan for their futures by enjoying today," *Chicago Tribune*, Sunday, 10 Oct., 1993.
2. Thomas L. Friedman, *The Lexus and the Olive Tree* (New York: Anchor Books/Random House, Inc., 2000) 7, 9.

Chapter 4

1. This journey was published in the book *The Fragile Curtain*, which was awarded The Christopher Award for work upholding the highest of human values. See page 132 for more details.
2. Wayne Muller, *Sabbath: Finding Rest, Renewal, and Delight in our Busy Lives* (New York, Bantam Books/Random House, Inc., 1999) 36.
3. Muller, *ibid.*
4. Marva J. Dawn, *Keeping the Sabbath Wholly: Ceasing, Resting, Embracing, Feasting* (Grand Rapids, Mich., Wm. B. Eerdmans Publishing Co., 1989) 50.
5. Muller, *Sabbath*, 38.

Chapter 7

1. Robert Banks, *Redeeming the Routines: Bringing Theology to Life* (Wheaton, Ill., Victor Books/SP Publications, Inc., 1993).

Chapter 8

1. "Safe Haven: Safe for Whom?" *U.S. Committee for Refugees*. Bill Frelick, 1995. USCR Articles, 2001 <http://222.refugees.org/world/articles/safehavens_wrs95.htm>.
2. "Safe Havens, Broken Promises," *Worldwide Refugee Information*. Bill Frelick, 1998. USCR Articles, 2001 <http://www.refugees.org/world/articles/safehavens_98.htm>.

 **Karen Mains** is a prolific author and an articulate communicator whose national prizewinning books address deep spiritual issues. Most of her creative works have been birthed out of personal experience as a pastor's wife and her many active years in radio and television broadcasting with The Chapel of the Air Ministries.

Her travels through barrios and refugee camps in Central America, Southeast Asia, the Middle East, and Africa resulted in her book *The Fragile Curtain*, which won the 1982 Christopher Award given to writers, producers, and directors whose works affirm the highest values of the human spirit and are representative of the best achievements in their fields. Since then, in the publishing of more than a dozen books, Karen has been the recipient of many other awards, including three Christian Booksellers' Gold Medallions.

Widely experienced in administrative leadership, Karen is now a member of the executive team of Mainstay Ministries, and her eight-year service on the board of InterVarsity Christian Fellowship culminated in being elected the first woman chairperson of that committee (1993–1995).

She and her husband, David, have been married for 40 years and live in the suburbs of Chicago. As the parents of four grown children, they are highly committed to Christian family values and are eagerly sharing their experience with the next generation, their growing clan of grandchildren.

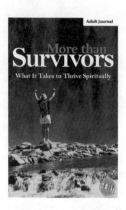

Do You Want to Be More than
Just a Spiritual Survivor?

WANT TO really thrive as a Christian?

Delve deeper into the topics and character heroes of this book through the *More than Survivors* Adult Journal. It will take you on a 50-Day Spiritual Adventure that explores more relevant scriptures, personal application steps, and God's truth in fun, practical, and life-changing ways.

This companion book to *Soul Alert* helps you avoid mediocrity and leads you, step by step, toward becoming a victorious, Christlike alien and stranger in this world. Give it a try and become *more* than a survivor!

To order, call Mainstay Church Resources toll-free at 1-800-224-2735 (U.S.) or 1-800-461-4114 (Canada). Or visit our website at www.teamsundays.org.

Make Sunday the Best Day of Your Week!

IN THIS insightful, encouraging, and delightful book, best-selling author Karen Mains challenges Christians to celebrate Sunday with a Sabbath heart—to make the Lord's Day so special that it brings days of anticipation . . . and so meaningful that it continues to nurture for three days afterward.

Making Sunday Special will help you and your family restore "the rhythm of the sacred" and fall in love anew with the day of rest and with Jesus Christ, the Lord of the Sabbath.

To order, call Mainstay Church Resources toll-free at 1-800-224-2735 (U.S.) or 1-800-461-4114 (Canada). Or visit our website at www.teamsundays.org.

THE FRAGILE CURTAIN

KAREN BURTON MAINS

Enter the World of Aliens and Strangers . . .

IN THE spring of 1980, Karen Mains made a traveling survey of the refugee camps of the world. She went to interpret the pain and suffering of these people; instead, they showed her the meaning of her own life—and of ours.

In this deeply moving book, Karen invites all of us to live through this experience with her, to look at our own lives: to celebrate the joy and the blessing and to be thankful that, despite sorrow and suffering, we dare to begin again.

To order, call Mainstay Church Resources toll-free at 1-800-224-2735 (U.S.) or 1-800-461-4114 (Canada). Or visit our website at www.teamsundays.org.

Hungry Souls

A "Next-to-the-best" Approach to Mentoring

**Are you a believer who hungers
for spiritual growth?**

**Searching for a wise spiritual mentor
but having trouble finding one?**

I F SO, Mainstay now offers a unique opportunity.
You see, many longtime church members, even
pastors and church leaders, are in the same situation.
They need someone to help them along the way—
someone with experience and training who prays for
and guides them in the disciplines of spiritual life.

Hungry Souls consists of a rare team of men and
women who have spent their lives both developing
tools for spiritual growth and experiencing the stretching that comes from honestly seeking God. Some of
these serve on church staffs in spiritual formation
responsibilities; all are trained and accredited. Through
centuries-old and contemporary tried-and-tested spiritual growth tools (or disciplines), these team members
work with Christians to develop depth and accountability that combines tenderness with firmness.

Aspects of Hungry Souls include:

- *God's Sacred Rhythms,* a bimonthly newsletter (6 issues/year)
- The website www.hungrysouls.org
- A weekly meditation page: www.thisquietplace.org
- "Soulish Food," a short, regular e-letter
- Monthly teleconference workshops on the spiritual disciplines
- Concentrated spiritual growth retreats around the U.S. and Canada
- Spiritual pilgrimages under the leadership of Hungry Souls team members
- Training for people who desire to be spiritual mentors
- Bibliographies of books, tools, and courses
- Retreat and spiritual growth material for small groups and church events
- Consultations on finding spiritual mentors

Visit our website, www.hungrysouls.org, scheduled to open in January 2002. For more detailed information, or to order an introductory copy of God's Sacred Rhythms, *call toll-free 1-800-224-2735 (U.S.) or 1-800-461-4114 (Canada).*